Mending the Broken Dialogue
Military Advice and
Presidential Decision-Making

COUNCIL *on*
FOREIGN
RELATIONS

DISCUSSION PAPER

Mending the Broken Dialogue
Military Advice and
Presidential Decision-Making

Janine A. Davidson
Emerson T. Brooking
Benjamin J. Fernandes

December 2016

The Council on Foreign Relations (CFR) is an independent, nonpartisan membership organization, think tank, and publisher dedicated to being a resource for its members, government officials, business executives, journalists, educators and students, civic and religious leaders, and other interested citizens in order to help them better understand the world and the foreign policy choices facing the United States and other countries. Founded in 1921, CFR carries out its mission by maintaining a diverse membership, with special programs to promote interest and develop expertise in the next generation of foreign policy leaders; convening meetings at its headquarters in New York and in Washington, DC, and other cities where senior government officials, members of Congress, global leaders, and prominent thinkers come together with CFR members to discuss and debate major international issues; supporting a Studies Program that fosters independent research, enabling CFR scholars to produce articles, reports, and books and hold roundtables that analyze foreign policy issues and make concrete policy recommendations; publishing Foreign Affairs, the preeminent journal on international affairs and U.S. foreign policy; sponsoring Independent Task Forces that produce reports with both findings and policy prescriptions on the most important foreign policy topics; and providing up-to-date information and analysis about world events and American foreign policy on its website, CFR.org.

The Council on Foreign Relations takes no institutional positions on policy issues and has no affiliation with the U.S. government. All views expressed in its publications and on its website are the sole responsibility of the author or authors.

For further information about CFR or this paper, please write to the Council on Foreign Relations, 58 East 68th Street, New York, NY 10065, or call Communications at 212.434.9888. Visit CFR's website, www.cfr.org.

The views presented are those of the authors and do not necessarily represent the views of the Department of the Navy, Department of the Army, or any other component of the Department of Defense.

Contents

Acronyms

AOR	area of responsibility
BPLAN	base plan
CAP	crisis action planning
CCMD	combatant command
CENTCOM	U.S. Central Command
CIA	Central Intelligence Agency
CONPLAN	concept plan
DC	deputies committee
FSI	Foreign Service Institute
FSO	Foreign Service officer
IPC	interagency policy committee
IPOC	interagency planning options cell
IPOG	Iraq Policy and Operations Group
JCS	Joint Chiefs of Staff
JSOC	Joint Special Operations Command
NSC	National Security Council
NSPD	National Security Presidential Directive
OPLAN	operation plan
OSD	Office of the Secretary of Defense
PDD	Presidential Decision Directive
PC	principals committee
PME	professional military education
TPFDD	time-phased force and deployment data
USAID	U.S. Agency for International Development

Introduction

As commander in chief of the armed forces, the president of the United States bears great responsibility in determining when and how to use military force. To make such decisions, the president requires a clear understanding of the risks, costs, and likely outcome of a military intervention. Because many presidents and senior civilian appointees lack deep operational military experience, they rely on senior military advisors to provide viable, realistic, and timely advice to inform these critical decisions. Unfortunately, what the military leadership provides is often not what presidents are looking for.

Whereas civilians expect a collaborative dialogue in which multiple options are presented to them over a short period of time, military officers are taught to deliver their "best military advice" after developing a detailed plan. This process, as codified in joint doctrine, assumes the president will provide specific guidance, including end states that clearly articulate the president's strategic intent, before detailed planning begins. To ensure that the option is viable—that the recommended course of action can be resourced from available forces and will achieve the perceived objective—this process also incorporates time-consuming war-gaming and analysis. Doing so takes much longer than civilians expect and can be stymied when presidents and their advisors are unable to provide the sort of detailed guidance the military expects. Meanwhile, the president cannot determine the best guidance and end state without first understanding the costs, risks, and benefits each option entails. This chicken-and-egg dilemma is a perennial feature of civil-military decision-making.

Although colorful reports and tell-all memoirs often attribute decision-making friction to clashes of personality, much of this tension originates from deeper institutional and cultural drivers. Military expectations about civil-military relations, war planning, and best military advice arise from a culture of military professionalism that has ingrained these expectations in its educational and institutional processes. Meanwhile, many senior civilian leaders, hailing largely from legal and academic backgrounds, are inclined to view national security policy as a Socratic exercise that blends rigorous debate and consensus-building.[1] If left unchecked, these divergent expectations can undermine presidential decision-making and lead to poor operational outcomes—even strategic failure.

This disconnect has been amplified in recent decades by a shift in the character of the national security challenges that confront the United States. With the exception of the 1991 Persian Gulf War, American policymakers have increasingly struggled to respond to simmering crises, in which gradually emerging complexities evade the traditional military planning process while political realities rule out any quick-fire answers. Examples include the crisis in the Balkans, conflict in Afghanistan, the Syrian civil war, and the deterioration of the Libyan state.

Developing useful, varied military options requires collaborative and respectful civil-military dialogue at multiple levels. It calls for a high-level focus on national security team-building across and within agencies, along with the preparation of incoming political appointees; clear White House guidance; updates to military planning doctrine and establishment of standing coordinating groups, coupled with more appreciation for informal interagency collaboration; adoption of more efficient communications protocols; and changes to the education of the next generation of military and Foreign Service officers. The challenges that confront the United States are rapidly evolving. In order to keep pace, the system of military advice needs to evolve as well.

How the Bureaucracy Goes to War

"Where you stand depends on where you sit."
—Rufus E. Miles, aide to Presidents Eisenhower, Kennedy, and Johnson,
in "The Origin and Meaning of Miles' Law"

Although the president wields ultimate authority over the use of military force, a series of complex institutions determines which, and how many, options the president receives. These institutions are the product of bureaucratic horse-trading, stubbornness, and chance. The modern national security system owes its structure to two pieces of legislation. The first, the National Security Act of 1947, sought to align the United States' range of military capabilities and authorities with its superpower-sized responsibilities. Following years of contentious debate between the Departments of the Army and the Navy, the act created the Department of the Air Force, as well as a coordinating Department of Defense and secretary of defense. The uniformed chiefs of each service convened to form the Joint Chiefs of Staff (JCS), supported by the Joint Staff. Separately, the act also created the National Security Council (NSC) to centralize the creation of national security policy, as well as the Central Intelligence Agency (CIA). Over time, as parts of this system proved untenable, a series of amendments in 1949 downgraded the military services from cabinet-level positions, removed the joint chiefs from the statutory NSC, strengthened the Department of Defense, and authorized additional personnel for a Joint Staff struggling to overcome the parochialism of the military services.[2]

Further reform would wait four decades. The 1986 Goldwater-Nichols Department of Defense Reorganization Act sought to address long-standing failures in military service coordination. It was inspired, in part, by lessons from the failed Iran hostage rescue operation of 1979 and 1983 invasion of Grenada, both of which revealed a severe lack of coordination among the services.[3] Goldwater-Nichols stripped the chairman of the JCS and the service chiefs of direct command authority. The new chain of command ran from the president through the secretary of defense to each unified combatant commander. The JCS assumed a coordinating and advisory function both within the Pentagon and to the White House. Although all combatant commanders around the globe now reported directly to the secretary of defense, the chairman of the JCS was designated as the principal military advisor to the president, a statutory relationship outside the operational chain of command.

Even as the national security establishment has evolved beyond the expectations of its creators, it remains characterized by fierce struggles over resources and authorities. In a system of roughly three million appointed officials, government professionals, and uniformed service members, only the president enjoys a degree of immunity from the influences of infighting and parochialism. In the words of Amy Zegart, "Presidents are the closest embodiment of national interest in the American political system."[4] This is a classic principal-agent problem: although the president is the ultimate principal, enactment of presidential decisions requires the advice of and action by a diverse set of agents, each with its own interests and incentives as well as its needed expertise.

Today, the principal actors in military force decisions are the NSC staff, the secretary of defense, the JCS, and combatant commanders. Although the president is the ultimate arbiter of the options presented, how the president defines the authority and relative influence of these actors sets the stage for how well these actors will work together to bring the best possible advice forward. Although there are many other formal and informal actors in this process, including other agencies, it is these principal actors in the Pentagon and the White House who bear the most responsibility in crafting and debating military options.

THE NATIONAL SECURITY COUNCIL

The NSC includes six statutory members—the president, vice president, secretary of state, secretary of defense, secretary of the treasury, and national security advisor—and two statutory advisors, the chairman of the JCS and the director of national intelligence. In practice, NSC meetings are coordinated by the national security advisor and

attended by additional relevant department secretaries, agency directors, and senior White House officials managing the issue under
discussion. When the president is absent, this group becomes the
principals committee (PC). Many significant policy decisions are
delegated to the deputies committee (DC), chaired by the deputy
national security advisor and attended by deputies of relevant departments and agencies.

Ideally, topical and regional interagency policy committees (IPCs),
which operate at the assistant secretary level, are intended to provide
the main forum for interagency coordination, responding to DC taskings and elevating issues to the DC for direction as necessary. The PC,
DC, and IPCs often need to operate through consensus because each
department reports directly to the president. Only the president or the
head of a department or agency can order that department or agency
to do something. The NSC staff of nearly four hundred appointees and
professionals orchestrates this work in support of the president.[5]

Despite its centrality in the modern national security system, the
NSC began life as a legislative afterthought. Its charter was vague: "to
advise the president with respect to the integration of domestic, foreign,
and military policies."[6] Despite the NSC's broad mission, Congress
was granted little oversight of the NSC's size and structure.[7] Harry S.
Truman, recognizing the NSC's potential, relocated its staff from the
State Department to the White House.[8] Dwight D. Eisenhower, having
learned to appreciate the usefulness of a general staff during his time as
supreme allied commander, institutionalized the NSC and carved out
a potent role for the national security advisor.[9] Together, Truman and
Eisenhower empowered the NSC, shaping it into a tool that no future
president could do without.

Virtually every president has tried to do without the NSC. John F.
Kennedy ran against the Eisenhower NSC bureaucracy, promptly slash-
ing its staff by a third—before gradually restoring and expanding it after
the failed Bay of Pigs invasion.[10] As national security advisor, Henry
Kissinger inherited an NSC staff of one hundred and left with a staff
of one hundred and fifty. Likewise, National Security Advisor Condo-
leezza Rice downsized the NSC by a third early in George W. Bush's
presidency but departed her post with 50 percent more staff than she
had started with.[11] President Barack Obama leaves office with an NSC
staff of roughly four hundred.[12] Regardless of presidential intent, the
future NSC staff is unlikely to shrink.

While presidents may encounter difficulty in reducing the size of the NSC, they exercise enormous discretion in determining how the NSC operates. This flexibility ensures that NSC staff meets the president's needs, but it also creates a situation in which personalities can have an outsize effect on how the NSC operates.[13] The ultimate currency is a personal connection with the president, as well as an intuitive sense of the president's positions.[14]

THE SECRETARY OF DEFENSE

Although the secretary of defense wields great influence in today's national security system, the position did not begin this way. In 1947, the secretary of defense lacked a dedicated staff and was hopelessly outgunned by the State Department.[15] Although the 1949 amendments helped to create the Office of the Secretary of Defense (OSD), Pentagon civilians did not assert centralized control until 1960, when Robert S. McNamara became secretary. McNamara hired scores of ambitious young civilian deputies, consolidated service procurement under his authority, and largely superseded the State Department in many foreign policy and use-of-force decisions.[16] While some powers atrophied after McNamara's departure, the secretary of defense and the OSD continue to play a central role in the military options process.

As the defense enterprise has grown, so has the role of the secretary of defense. No longer simply a manager of the department, the secretary also needs to be a skilled negotiator, able to ease the relationship between Pentagon civilians and uniformed personnel. According to a former senior Pentagon official, "We want OSD and the Joint Staff to be on the same page before we go across the river. Because if we're on the same page, we have two votes, and if we're not on the same page, we'll cancel each other out."[17] Additionally, close relations with the State Department have become increasingly important for the Pentagon as the United States faces few security challenges solvable by military force alone.

Although many senior defense officials—similar to their NSC peers—have civilian backgrounds, defense civilians often take positions closer to the uniformed military officials in their assessments and institutional sympathies. This seeming civil-military cohesion belies the contentious debate and civil-military maneuvering over military options and strategic priorities that takes place inside the Pentagon.

THE JOINT CHIEFS OF STAFF

In contrast to the secretary of defense, the influence of the JCS and Joint Staff has generally declined from its World War II peak. The JCS was established in 1942 to provide a unified military voice while coordinating with U.S. allies. It comprised the chiefs of the functional services, each of whom exercised almost total command from Washington to the warzone. This arrangement, combined with its lack of a formal charter, gave the JCS essentially unlimited power in prosecuting the war.[18] After peace was declared, the structure of the joint chiefs became the focus of a long and contentious debate.

Although the chiefs were expected to make hard decisions on behalf of the entire military, doing so could easily rob them of the support of their own service—in turn, destroying their effectiveness.[19] As Zegart writes, "Ironically, the very importance of the joint chiefs of staff guaranteed it would be poorly designed to serve the national interest."[20] The Goldwater-Nichols act sought to address this issue by removing the service chiefs from the chain of command, which unintentionally endangered their relevance. Today, service chiefs wield far less influence over current operations and national strategy despite their position as JCS members.

The chairman of the JCS, also absent from the chain of command, nonetheless holds a powerful tool as independent military advisor to the president. The use of this relationship—and the relative influence—can vary drastically from one chairman to the next. Lack of Pentagon allies, an overbearing secretary of defense, or a poor personal connection with the president can render the chairman effectively invisible.

Today, the JCS includes the chairman; vice chairman; service chiefs of the U.S. Army, Air Force, Navy, and Marine Corps; and, since 2012, chief of the National Guard Bureau. While the chairman serves as the principal military advisor to the president and the secretary of defense, all JCS members are military advisors by law and may respond to a request from or voluntarily submit advice or opinions to the president, the secretary of defense, or NSC staff. JCS members may also submit their independent recommendations to Congress.

The Joint Staff works for the chairman and vice chairman and includes the traditional military staff sections (J1 through J8) covering everything from personnel and training to intelligence, strategy, and operations. It supports the chairman's advisory role and coordinates the military services' efforts to organize, train, and equip their services.[21] Within the planning process, the Joint Staff is intended to be the

glue that binds everything: officers on the Joint Staff interface directly
with OSD officials, coordinate with individual combatant commanders, and oversee global force management.[22]

In practice, the Joint Staff struggles to meet its diverse responsibilities. Much of the regional expertise needed to inform the options
desired by the White House resides with individual combatant commands (CCMDs), not the Joint Staff. Consequently, the NSC staff is
often tempted to bypass the Joint Staff entirely; indeed, the Joint Staff
often simply transfers planning responsibility to the CCMD when it
receives a request for options from the White House. In the process,
however, the president may get only one regional commander's perspective without other, crucial contextualizing information that only the
Joint Staff has—such as the global availability of forces or the risk that
an unplanned deployment might pose to other theaters of operation.

Ultimately, the JCS and Joint Staff are best considered interpreters,
translating the political guidance of the White House into useable directives for the unified CCMDs. There is an expectation—only sometimes
fulfilled—that the JCS should take an active role in the deliberative process. As one former national security advisor said, "If the Joint Staff
wants to have a dialogue with the CCMDs, that's great! But the Joint
Staff needs . . . the capacity to develop options."[23]

COMBATANT COMMANDS

Little military planning can occur without the cooperation of the
CCMDs. These are the geographic and functional commands that
actively manage deployed U.S. forces, including their disposition
within a given area of responsibility (AOR); they will become the operational command if war breaks out in their area. The strategy, plans,
and program directorate of each CCMD—known as the J5—develops
the concepts of operations or more detailed plans that determine the
required capabilities to fulfill the CCMD's mission. However, the J5
lacks the broader view of worldwide force disposition or strategy; its
planning assumes, often erroneously, that the Joint Staff will prioritize
its demands over all others' when and if the time comes to fight.

Since the 1986 Goldwater-Nichols act, combatant commanders have
enjoyed operational autonomy over their AORs, collaborating with the
Joint Staff to fully vet and assess military options. However, this has

been countered by a strengthening of the statutory powers of OSD to compel a detailed civilian review of military plans before they are sent to the secretary of defense for approval.[24] Although the resultant process is thorough, it is also slow, adding weeks and months to a procedure that was never fast to begin with.

CCMDs are largely insulated from the political and economic considerations driving senior policymakers. According to one former combatant commander, "I've got my given area, my military thing . . . but in order to be successful in anything that counts, you've got to have strong coordination between State and the Pentagon at a minimum, plus all the other actors. Where that comes to a large degree is in the [deputies committee], but the combatant commands aren't in the DC."[25] The result of this institutional arrangement is that combatant commanders, unaware of global requirements, may produce military options that require an unrealistically high commitment of forces, which they reasonably consider to be their best military advice on how to achieve the perceived objective.

One response has been to directly incorporate combatant commanders into high-level decision-making. George W. Bush used this method during his second term, as he scheduled regular video conferences with the commander of U.S. Central Command (CENTCOM) to receive updates on the Iraq War.[26] Yet, even this decision had institutional ramifications, leaving many critical NSC actors in the dark and circumventing the interpretative and advising functions of the Joint Staff and the OSD. In a system so large and complex, it can be tempting to skip seemingly superfluous layers of bureaucracy. Later, when it comes time for implementation, which requires detailed insight on force availability, logistical timelines, and the like, it becomes clear just how important those layers are.

Culture Clash

"Are they suspicious of my politics? Do they resent that I never served in the military? Do they think because I'm young that I don't see what they're doing?"
—Barack Obama, as quoted in *Duty*

"The military man tends to see himself as the perennial victim of civilian warmongering. It is the people and the politicians . . . who start wars. It is the military who have to fight them."
—Samuel P. Huntington, *The Soldier and the State*

The U.S. military operates under a system of civilian control. This belief in civilian authority, deeply ingrained in the philosophies of the Founding Fathers, has stood virtually unchallenged for 240 years. But the definition of civilian control can be the subject of heated debate.

The cause of such divergent expectations can be traced to fundamental differences in civilian and institutional military cultures. Although the United States was founded in a tradition of part-time militiamen and citizen soldiers, the military had developed a professional core by the start of World War I and was wholly professionalized with the introduction of the all-volunteer force in 1973. Career military personnel now exist in a world apart from 99.5 percent of American society: they go to different schools, live and work in a specialized system of promotions and deployments, and often belong to successive generations of the same families.[27] While subordinate to civilian leaders, military officers are taught that their professional judgment should be respected once the fighting starts.[28]

By contrast, many of the men and women who find their way to senior NSC positions and departmental appointments do so by excelling in the think tank community, academia, or the legal or business professions, as well as by demonstrating political savvy. Although they are often graduates of the world's finest universities, they are hardly bound by a common curriculum. Only rarely will these policymakers have had prior exposure to the military or Pentagon before they find themselves working with military professionals with fifteen to forty years of service. Although many of these civilians lack military experience, they bring knowledge of broader political and strategic concerns. They will want to develop and guide military options that align with this broader national security thinking.

The mystique of military culture can also serve to put civilians on the defensive. Former Secretary of State Madeleine Albright, recalling her early NSC meetings with Colin Powell, then chairman of the JCS, felt that Powell could come off as the only "grown-up" in the room. As she put it, "Somebody walks in with a uniform and has a chest full of medals and is the hero of the Western world . . . there is a certain something about a winning military commander."[29] Meanwhile, a former NSC staffer described how this divide cuts both ways:

> The average NSC staffer is a whiz kid who's thirty-two years old or something . . . So I'm thirty, you know, I went to Harvard, Yale, Princeton, Stanford, whatever, and there I am, and there's this one-star general and he's at least forty-five. I'm smarter than he is, why do I have to listen to this crap from him? And from [the general's] point of view, this is not the president, who is this punk? This kid who went to private school and then the Ivy League— he's never deployed, never been shot at, never done nothing! His time overseas is probably in the French Riviera.[30]

This difference of experience, coupled with divergent views of the deliberative process, can prime military leaders and civilian appointees for conflict before they even meet.

THE PROFESSIONAL MILITARY ETHIC

Although the first edition of Samuel Huntington's *The Soldier and the State* is now nearly sixty years old, it remains a foundational text in the education of military officers. "The modern officer corps is a professional body and the modern military officer is a professional man," Huntington wrote.[31] Because of the technical expertise required to plan and conduct modern warfare, soldiers need to be wholly devoted to their training, removing themselves from society at large. Such "management of violence" is not an art or a talent but a hard-learned skill—in fact, a "profession."[32]

For Huntington, while civilians should set national policy, the particulars of military campaigns should be left to the professionals who understand them best. This equilibrium is called objective control, and in this system, civilian leaders furnish the "dynamic, purposive element to state policy." The military, meanwhile, represents the "passive, instrumental means."[33] The politician speaks and then the soldier acts. It is a series of orders, not a conversation.

However, this is a series of orders that civilians are often unprepared to give at the level of detail the Huntington model presumes—and a degree of control the military is unwilling to relinquish. When civilian leaders probe for more information or choose to commit forces without articulating a clear end state, they are seen to be meddling—overstepping the bounds of objective control and micromanaging decisions that the professionals should be making. For a generation of military officers, the Vietnam War represented the height of such civilian interference, colored by images of Lyndon B. Johnson's obsessing over the targeting lists for individual air strikes.[34]

As a repudiation of the Vietnam War and a clear endorsement of the line between civilian and military authorities, in 1984, Secretary of Defense Caspar Weinberger gave a speech titled "The Uses of Military Power." In it, he laid out six prerequisites for the use of military force: that the conflict be vital to U.S. interests, that there be a clear intention of "winning," that there be clearly defined political and military objectives, that the size of the military force be continually reassessed, that this action receive the support of the U.S. Congress and American people, and that such force be used as a last resort.[35] As chairman of the JCS in the early 1990s, Colin Powell reaffirmed, updated, and infused joint doctrine with Weinberger's principles, and the resulting doctrine came to dominate the professional military education system.

Adherents of the Powell Doctrine and objective control often characterize the 1991 Persian Gulf War as an ideal example of civil-military relations in action. The United States fought Iraq with a large and well-equipped force that took months to deploy, based on a fully vetted plan, firm domestic support, and a civilian leadership that left campaign planning and mission termination almost entirely to the discretion of the military commander, General Norman Schwarzkopf. As his chief of staff would later recall, "Schwarzkopf was never second-guessed by civilians, and that's the way it ought to work."[36] Casualties were light; the fighting lasted only one hundred hours. In some ways, it resembled a football game as much as a war, with a clear winner and loser. At the end of the match, the quarterbacks signed a cease-fire, shook hands, and went home, albeit committed to a no-fly zone that would last until the 2003 Iraq invasion.

Dig deeper and the results look less rosy. Schwarzkopf entered cease-fire negotiations with neither clear guidance from the White House nor diplomatic instructions from the State Department. No senior civilian officials were present, nor were any representatives from the Air Force during the negotiations. Among his concessions, Schwarzkopf infamously allowed the Iraqi army to continue flying helicopters, inadvertently enabling the killing of thousands of Shia and Kurdish rebels.[37]

In reality, military leaders cannot be the silent, detached professionals envisioned by Huntington nor can they enjoy the clarity demanded by Powell. Instead, military operations and policy should have a continuous, interactive relationship. This requires a strong and iterative civil-military dialogue at all levels.

LOST IN TRANSLATION

When military and civilian officials discuss military options, they often lack a common vocabulary. This is due, in part, to the Pentagon acronym soup that is second nature to military officers but often alien to newly appointed civilians. It is also due to the precise military definitions attached to certain commonly used words and terms.

Where military and civilian officials are least likely to see eye-to-eye are on basic issues of speed, scale, and logistics. According to Major General William Hix, a former chief planning officer in the Joint Staff, "There are simple laws of physics at play in military planning."[38] This science determines how quickly a brigade or battalion can deploy to a given theater, how many soldiers will be required to adequately accomplish a task, or how much logistical support is required of an Air Force squadron. It also determines how the allocation of resources to a particular region will change global force posture and thus shift the deployment and contingency plans across the entire Pentagon planning apparatus.

This ripple effect changes presidential options, usually limiting them in one theater in order to execute in another. Such tradeoffs based on logistical and operational realities need to be clearly articulated to civilian leadership for the president to clearly understand the tradeoffs at stake, issue any guidance, or make decisions over use of force.

Military advisors are also extremely cautious in their estimates of the number of troops required to accomplish a given mission. Johnson, arguing with the JCS over troop levels for Vietnam, complained that his generals had no understanding of strategy beyond "more men!"[39] Likewise, the administration of Bill Clinton was "paralyzed" by 1992 estimates that it would require four hundred thousand troops to intervene in Bosnia, while Army Chief of Staff Eric Shinseki was famously chastised in 2003 by Secretary of Defense Donald Rumsfeld for testifying that force levels allotted to the invasion and stabilization of Iraq would be inadequate to the task at hand.[40] This tendency toward large force requirements, which can appear manipulative to suspicious civilians, arises from the professional military ethic. As Huntington writes, the military officer's professional responsibility "leads him to feel that if he errs in his estimate, it should be on the side of overstating the threat."[41]

Nowhere is this issue of physics more apparent than in the question of enablers—the logistical tail required for any long-term deployment of combat forces. Although the requirement for enablers is second nature to any junior military planner, neither civilian education nor experience is likely to teach the importance of enablers. Journalist Bob Woodward recounts how, following months of deliberation among Obama's NSC regarding 2009 troop levels for Afghanistan, the Pentagon requested 4,500 enablers above the agreed-upon total. Obama declared, "I'm done with this!" while his deputy national security advisor expressed doubt that 4,500 enablers were really "necessary."[42] Secretary of Defense Robert Gates, meanwhile, grew so furious at this second-guessing that he came "closer to resigning that day than at any other time" in his five-year tenure.[43]

Civilian and military expectations also diverge sharply on the question of risk. To the president and civilian advisors, risk is inextricably linked to the profile and domestic political opinion of a given military action. By contrast, military planners—raised on the Powell Doctrine—will seek to meet every conflict with overwhelming force, ensuring faster victory with fewer casualties and lower financial costs. The fact that troops face less individual risk in a military action as their numbers increase is taken as elementary to military professionals but may seem paradoxical to civilians who assume fewer troops exposed to combat means fewer casualties. Thus, this planning logic often goes unappreciated by civilian officials, who prefer the lightest and least visible footprint possible.[44]

As a result of these divergent perspectives on military physics and risk, the military will hesitate to provide options for contingencies without a clearly achievable end state. In the absence of options from their military advisors, civilians may concoct their own. James Steinberg, former deputy national security advisor to Clinton (later deputy secretary of state under Obama), recalled how the chairman of the JCS "simply did not want to provide options" in the late 1990s as the Clinton administration debated how to counter the emerging threat of transnational terrorism, including an expanding al-Qaeda.[45] Consequently, the Clinton administration largely delegated counterterrorism duties to the CIA, which faced different legal parameters and cost-benefit-risk considerations.

The Problem With Military Advice

> *"Elected officials are hard-wired to ask for options first and then reverse-engineer objectives. And the military is hard-wired to do exactly the opposite."*
> —General Martin E. Dempsey, former chairman of the JCS,
>   as quoted in *Joint Forces Quarterly*

It is 3 a.m., and the president receives a phone call about a crisis—a sudden provocation in the South China Sea or a Middle East nation sliding into chaos. According to both Hollywood movies and established military doctrine, the president will huddle in the Situation Room with senior civilian and military advisors before emerging, clear-eyed and filled with resolve, to announce a response and issue guidance to waiting military commanders. Military planners translate this strategic guidance into concrete action. The president and NSC are left to watch as the U.S. military machine grinds to life, carriers shifting course and brigades wheeling into position. Civilian control and military execution work in perfect tandem: an impressive display of American resolve and power. It is also a fairy tale.

Presidents are not omniscient. If U.S. intelligence agencies and CCMDs struggle to piece together the facts on the ground, senior civilians sitting thousands of miles away in the Situation Room will be even less confident in their ability to make a good decision. Before the president issues strategic guidance, he or she will want to understand possible choices and the costs, benefits, and risks of each option: the capabilities available and how they can be used, their effect on other U.S. interests, and the potential financial costs and risk of casualties. Military advisors cannot answer these questions off the tops of their heads. Military education and doctrine describe a detailed and thorough process designed to ensure the military can generate, deploy, and sustain enough trained and ready military forces to fulfill any objective the president might request. By consequence, this process is slow and ingrained with a level of detail civilians do not expect or think they need.

A former senior military planner in the Joint Staff describes these divergent expectations as two different approaches to analyzing a book. Civilians, he says, want to read the first chapter and then ask questions about it. They will do the same in chapters two and three, journeying through the book such that, by the time they reach the conclusion, they have a good sense of how everything fits together. By contrast, the military is trained to scan the table of contents, find the chapters most relevant to the conclusion, and then outline and diagram them with extraordinary detail.[46]

When forced to give an estimate without the benefit of the regular planning process, military advisors will respond as conservatively as possible. A former member of State Department policy planning staff expressed his frustration at the choices the Pentagon provided: "The military will give you two options: nonintervention or World War III."[47]

Although the military planning system historically has been out of sync with the needs of civilian leaders, this tension has been stretched further by an evolution in the security challenges that the United States faces. Scenarios from the South China Sea to Syria can only be "managed," not solved outright. Such crises are fundamentally at odds with a planning process that assumes a limited deployment window and clearly articulated end states.

HOW MILITARY PLANNING WORKS

The Pentagon is constantly planning. In the normal planning process, known as deliberate planning, the president and secretary of defense task the military to build plans for an array of contingencies across the spectrum from "most likely" to "most dangerous." Most of these plans will never be executed, and none will unfold exactly as predicted. The real value of the planning process lies in its function as a rehearsal for the array of actors who may need to coordinate actions in a response. It is an adage often attributed to Eisenhower: "Plans are worthless, but planning is everything."[48]

This system is designed to refine broad, strategic guidance into granular layers. According to Joint Publication 5-0, "Joint Operation Planning," the process begins as the JCS receives a directive from the secretary of defense. Once the Joint Staff has reviewed and refined this guidance, it is submitted to the relevant CCMD, where the bulk of detailed analysis takes place. In time, the combatant commander returns to the Joint Staff with a recommended course of action, as well as potential alternatives. The Joint Staff reconciles the requirements of the proposed plan with the global pool of available forces and equipment and facilitates an assessment between OSD and the relevant CCMD. Although the cycle is concluded as the secretary of defense formally approves the plan, the process never ends. Each approved plan is subject to regular review.

It is curious to note that this planning process, as written into doctrine and approved by the chairman of the JCS, overtly inserts the chairman into the chain of command, which, by law, is intended to flow directly from the secretary of defense to the combatant commander. Given the Joint Staff's global perspective and access to worldwide readiness data, it should certainly have an important role in this process, but it is up to the secretary of defense to decide whether guidance to the combatant commander should be filtered or otherwise translated by the chairman and the Joint Staff. However the guidance is conveyed to the planning staff, it is important to keep open channels of communication back to OSD and the Joint Staff in order to avoid confusion and to promote a shared understanding of the problem being addressed.

In the event of a sudden emergency, the military shifts from a model of deliberate planning to crisis action planning (CAP). As a starting point, CAP uses the campaign and contingency plans developed in the deliberate planning process. If none exists for the problem at hand, the process begins with an expedited planning effort by the combatant commander that combines the normal planning elements with additional focus on immediate execution.

For the military, ideally all planning is predicated on clear strategic guidance, the instructions that—in theory—spring from NSC meetings following presidential decisions.[49] Weighty questions regarding strategic objectives and how the desired military end state contributes to a greater strategy are expected to be resolved before the Pentagon begins the work of resourcing and risk analysis.[50] Furthermore, although the doctrine expects combatant commanders to deliver multiple courses of action to meet a directed end state, time constraints often restrict thorough planning to a single preferred course of action, with less optimal—and less detailed—"high" and "low" variants. Senior civilians may wait weeks to receive a single viable course of action, and alternative end states are hardly considered at all.

A former senior Joint Staff planner describes the wishful scenario that is the logical conclusion of this doctrine: "The combatant commander [is going to] take a refined operations plan where all the big decisions have been made and present it to the president, and the president is going to say, 'I got it, combatant commander! Thanks a lot; I'll do what you say.'"[51] In reality, the president almost never does this. Civilians see these proposed plans as the start of a conversation, not the end. The president bears ultimate responsibility for any decision and so will rarely be willing to simply let the military do its thing.

Even if the president followed military doctrine to the letter and gave a clear end state to the combatant commander, this end state would likely contradict military expectations. As a former national security advisor explains, "Why would you want a process where you just sit there until some civilian, who has never seen combat, has not had the training you've had, comes and gives you guidance and you're going to accept that and immediately plan on that basis?"[52] A robust civil-military dialogue at the political and strategic levels may go against the tradition of the professional military ethic, but it would arguably serve to enhance military input in these crucial, early phases of deliberation, ultimately improving the planning process.

THE BANDWIDTH GAP

In the deliberate planning process, the Pentagon assesses each contingency in one of four levels of detail. The first is that of a commander's estimate, intended to explore possible courses of action in the broadest terms possible. The second is that of a base plan (BPLAN), which will include discussion of operational design and forces involved but will not include a computation of precise force levels and necessary redeployments. The final two levels, a concept plan (CONPLAN) and an operation plan (OPLAN), are lighter and heavier variants of a full-fledged war plan. They typically include time-phased force and deployment data (TPFDD), an intensive calculation of the troop movements and logistical support necessary to resource the plan.

The full process takes time. NSC staff and other civilian officials can grow frustrated with the perceived sluggishness of the Pentagon.

After all, the Pentagon has separate planning elements spread across numerous OSD offices, the Joint Staff, and each individual service component and CCMD; in 2013, CENTCOM alone employed over one hundred uniformed and civilian military planners.[53] Many of these elements exceed the size of the central planning offices of an entire civilian department. Thus, when a planning request is left unanswered for weeks, civilians can suspect that they are being "slow-rolled" by a Pentagon whose arcane processes provide a convenient excuse.

Yet, detailed planning really does take this long. Examining the hard questions of logistics necessary to develop a viable military option requires immense time and effort. Planners juggle many competing requests atop their daily obligations to develop plans for other potential scenarios or update plans for actual ongoing operations: the contingency plan for the Korean Peninsula should not skip its regular review, for instance. Any option that works its way through CCMD, JCS, and OSD to the secretary of defense should be realistic and almost immediately executable; otherwise, the military advice would be deficient.

Just as civilians may hold unrealistic expectations of the military's available bandwidth, the opposite is also true. Pentagon planning expects an extraordinary amount of participation from the "interagency"—representatives of the State Department, the U.S. Agency for International Development (USAID), the intelligence community, and other agencies—at every level of the planning process. If the military is stretched to fulfill the requirements of the deliberate planning process, overloaded civilian agencies, many of which lack even a basic planning staff, cannot provide expeditious support. In the words of a former national security advisor, "Nobody shows up for the planning. And therefore, you don't have the plans in place that prevent the crises and you end up doing crisis management."[54]

The challenge of the bandwidth gap is best illustrated by two NSC initiatives intended to address it: the 1997 Presidential Decision Directive 56 (PDD 56), "The Clinton Administration's Policy on Managing Complex Contingency Operations," and the 2005 National Security Presidential Directive 44 (NSPD 44), "Management of Interagency Efforts Concerning Reconstruction and Stabilization." PDD 56 was intended to formulate whole-of-government approaches to planning, following haphazard interagency coordination in Haiti, Panama, and Somalia, while NSPD 44 sought to improve coordination based on the lessons learned from the stability operations in Iraq and Afghanistan.[55] The limited effect of these directives demonstrates the depth of these systemic challenges.

PDD 56 elevated the level of seniority at which interdepartmental coordination occurred and required a political-military implementation plan in advance of a crisis; a dress rehearsal and interagency simulation before the plan was put into action; a thorough after-action report; and a new interagency training program for some mid-level government employees.[56] For all its ambition, however, implementation of PDD 56 faltered. Civilian agencies were loath to "militarize" their planning processes to emulate the Pentagon; they also lacked the resources to do so.[57] Although two dozen political-military implementation plans were drafted, the major 1999 Kosovo intervention and Bosnia stability planning remained strictly military, with civilians looped in on an ad hoc basis.[58] No agency accepted these changes willingly, and the incoming George W. Bush administration quickly wiped PDD 56 from the books.

In 2005, however, the Bush administration sought to institute its own interagency planning directive intended to address perceived failings in ensuring the stability of Iraq.[59] This directive, NSPD 44, firmly established the State Department as the lead agency in interagency coordination during stability operations, with a more active role in contingency planning.[60] Nonetheless, the level of authorized resources did not match the scope of this mandate. As well, the State Department office tasked with implementing the directive lacked the convening authority across agencies and even within the State Department itself. Although the Obama administration did not dismantle this system, it has not publicly issued directives to strengthen interagency planning.

PDD 56 and NSPD 44 suggest that lasting reform to interagency planning will require more than a presidential directive simply laying out a process. The limits of institutional bandwidth, combined with ingrained cultural differences among agencies, represent a deep, systemic challenge. For the Pentagon, the comprehensiveness of the regular planning process imposes constraints on the number of options that can be proposed at once, while civilian agencies lack the staff and resources to contribute to any planning process, much less lead one. Agencies expected to participate in a presidentially mandated planning process require commensurate resources—including more personnel for those agencies that lack planning staff—to participate productively. All parties require interagency training to promote shared expectations for planning in support of presidential decision-making. Moreover, representatives need to be empowered to freely explore ideas with their interagency partners.

THE SIMMERING CRISIS

The modern defense establishment arose from the Cold War as the president and executive agencies confronted a world of potential contingencies and rapid-reaction crises. What the nation now increasingly faces, however, are simmering crises that require continuous monitoring but whose complexity and uncertainty can overwhelm the regular planning process. Difficulty in planning for these crises is compounded by a lack of consensus over not only which tools or strategy might best address the problem but also whether it is in the nation's interests to act at all.

Simmering crises can generate a cascade of bad headlines that gradually infiltrate domestic U.S. politics. As demands for the White House to act build, the president will want to explore options. Unfortunately, the traditional military planning process, as discussed, is likely to produce only a single, viable course of action. As the president requests more options, the facts on the ground will continue to shift, eventually invalidating courses of action that have already been prepared.[61] Over time, the president, NSC staff, and the Pentagon can seem to be working incessantly without making much progress.

Relying on the traditional military planning process for simmering crises can eventually impose opportunity costs across the entire planning apparatus. Time spent responding to the latest political development diverts attention from the rest of the deliberate planning process and steady-state operations intended to advance other U.S. interests and prevent future crises. Military leaders worry that this resource-intensive planning loop focused on a single crisis can leave the Pentagon unprepared for or distracted from other potential threats.[62]

This dynamic is complicated further by issues of prioritization. The military prefers clear civilian tasking before it begins serious study of a contingency that commanders deem a low priority. Meanwhile, sensitive to leaks and domestic politics, the president and NSC staff may hesitate to formally request military options until they expect to authorize a military intervention. Political sensitivities can also result in orders to not plan for certain events, preventing combatant commanders and the Joint Staff from anticipating force requirements. This standoff can waste critical time in the early stages of a crisis. When the planning directive does come, it often comes with an unrealistically short deadline. As one retired senior military officer described it, "Well, we don't have a plan because you prevented us from planning!"[63]

The civil war in Syria stands as a clear example of a simmering crisis. Following guidance from the NSC, the secretary of defense and the Joint Staff initiated the CAP process in March 2011, during the early stages of Syria's disintegration.[64] U.S. Army Major Sean Carmody, in his study of early planning during the Syrian crisis, recalled how the NSC never formally expressed its intent to intervene directly. Consequently, "this lack of pre-decision directly caused the retention of integration by the NSC. By retaining this function, no organization, to include [CENTCOM], could effectively plan and integrate a whole-of-government approach for consideration."[65]

Because of deep uncertainty, senior White House civilians were reluctant to choose a specific course of action, which would necessarily involve relinquishing some of their control over the process to the agencies responsible for implementation. Instead, the NSC kept going back to the drawing board in search of options. This meant that the Pentagon kept up the CAP process in Syria for two years, continually revving a system that had been intended for quick strategy formation and implementation. Meanwhile, as Syria fragmented, many military options, built on political conditions that had ceased to exist, became unviable. They were, as the military might describe it, "OBE"—overtaken by events.[66]

Twenty-five months into the CAP process, as the U.S. Congress called for "real" military options, General Martin Dempsey, then chairman of the JCS, penned a public letter to Senator Carl Levin, then chairman of the Senate Armed Services Committee, articulating five possible military options in Syria.[67] Dempsey wrote, "The decision over whether to introduce military force is a political one that our Nation entrusts to its civilian leaders. I . . . understand that you deserve my best military advice on how military force *could* be used in order to decide whether it *should* be used."[68]

Dempsey's short, public letter signaled a dramatic departure from the typically quiet work of military planning and most planning products: it outlined five distinct options, each with a different end state along with the associated costs and risks. The letter, a cogent summation of a planning effort that had been running nonstop for two years, served to inform—and educate—lawmakers on the real limits of military force.

The Dempsey letter did not solve the crisis in Syria. It did, however, place the available military options in context. Although each option was premised on significant analysis, it was the short, clearly written document that many civilians had been waiting for. The options presented revealed complexity of the Syrian crisis: the available military options were costly, time-consuming, and ultimately inconclusive and unsatisfying. Those hoping for a quick fix were disappointed.

As the Syria crisis demonstrated, simmering crises can spin out over years while generating brief periods of intense policy debate based on news cycles, spikes in violence, personnel shifts, or other ephemeral events. Rough order-of-magnitude planning of the sort embodied by the Dempsey letter could be used as a model to help leaders understand what is possible and what is not. Ideally, military planning that clearly identifies multiple viable options, presented in clear language civilians can understand, will help presidents decide not only how, but if the United States should take international action—and at what cost. The challenge in developing such "back-of-the-envelope" ideas comes in ensuring that the options will be viable. Without reforms to the military planning process that can provide some level of confidence in this shorter time frame, military advisors will be loath to deliver such products to policymakers.

Civil-Military Friction and System Failure

"Not a single instance exists in which there was not some degree of friction between the White House and military in the planning and execution of conflict."
—Robert M. Gates, former secretary of defense, interview with author

Friction is an inevitable and important part of the policymaking process. However, too much or too little of it can sabotage civil-military dialogue.

The presidencies of Truman and Eisenhower were characterized by the growing powers of the NSC and the secretary of defense at the expense of a previously all-powerful JCS. Each dealt with highly visible military dissension over issues of spending cuts, bureaucratic centralization, strategy, and nuclear control. Although this military disapproval was often vocal, it did not represent an unhealthy civil-military dialogue so much as a dialogue that did not go the military's way. Here, the exception that proved the rule was General Douglas MacArthur's insubordination and subsequent firing by Truman during the Korean War.[69] It was MacArthur's abandonment by the professional military establishment as much as Truman's displeasure that sealed his fate. The MacArthur episode was an aberration, not a symptom, of civil-military relations.

Kennedy entered office distrustful of senior military leadership.[70] This distrust grew in the aftermath of the Bay of Pigs fiasco, as the joint chiefs had endorsed the failed plan, undermining the new president's confidence in military advice.[71] As a result, Kennedy's secretary of defense, Robert S. McNamara, asserted unprecedented control over the Pentagon, while Kennedy's selection of former Army Chief of Staff Maxwell Taylor as close aide and confidante largely superseded the military advisory role of the JCS. In time, top generals learned their lesson—they became more politicized. As the war in Vietnam worsened, many senior military leaders held their tongues, seeking to accumulate valuable political capital.[72] In 1965, Johnson told the assembled joint chiefs, "You're my team now; you're all Johnson men."[73] No one corrected him.

Following a dramatic increase in the power of the NSC staff under Richard Nixon, Gerald Ford, and Jimmy Carter, the Ronald Reagan administration sought to reduce its influence, devolving authorities to the Pentagon and State Department.[74] This stoked tensions between Secretary of State George Schultz and Secretary of Defense Caspar Weinberger that impeded the interagency process.[75] Schultz argued frequently for military intervention abroad; Weinberger and the Pentagon pushed back just as hard. As a former State Department appointee recalled, "The main message coming out of the Pentagon, meaning both the secretary of defense and the uniformed military—no space between them—was, 'Go away.'"[76]

Amid this conflict, Reagan remained largely hands-off in his management style. This bureaucratic dysfunction led to poor oversight and, in time, outcomes like the Iran-Contra scandal.[77] Only at the end of the Reagan administration did the system improve, as the NSC reasserted its authority and the national security advisor, secretary of defense, and secretary of state met daily for an informal consultation.[78]

The administrations of George H.W. Bush and Bill Clinton were characterized by two different civil-military dynamics. The Bush administration—staffed by seasoned veterans of the Nixon and Ford administrations—moved as close as the nation ever had to a model of objective control. When the Persian Gulf War began, decision-making power was delegated almost entirely to CENTCOM. Secretary of Defense Dick Cheney made only one significant interference in the conduct of the war—requisitioning aircraft to hunt Iraqi SCUD missile launchers targeting Israel—and provoked military resentment in the process.[79] The White House was similarly deferential in allowing CENTCOM to set the terms of the Iraqi cease-fire. While this decision respected military autonomy, it was not necessarily good strategy.

Under Clinton, civil-military relations were almost immediately combative.[80] The military cited the Powell Doctrine as a sacred text; NSC and State Department officials felt repeatedly stonewalled on the issue of humanitarian intervention in Bosnia.[81] Moreover, Clinton's early push for gays in the military lit a firestorm in the culturally conservative Pentagon as the JCS effectively threatened to resign.[82] In his advocacy for this policy shift, Lee Aspin, Clinton's first secretary of defense, effectively "lost the building."[83] The 1993 "Black Hawk Down" disaster in Somalia was the final straw, leading to angry recriminations between the White House and senior military leaders.[84] Although this civil-military tension would persist for most of Clinton's presidency, the lessons from Somalia directly informed the development of PDD 56, which dramatically improved interagency planning processes. Although PDD 56 was discarded by the George W. Bush administration, for many civilian and military leaders today, it remains a blueprint for more coordinated and informed interagency planning.[85]

Although George W. Bush had campaigned on a professed deference to the military, his administration instituted a system of civilian control as aggressive as any since Kennedy. As vice president, Dick Cheney largely co-opted the coordinating powers of the NSC, routing them through his office and informal patronage network. He recommended the appointment of his longtime associate, Donald Rumsfeld, as secretary of defense. In turn, Rumsfeld launched an energetic campaign of institutional reorganization, attempting to purge the JCS of its Clinton-appointed chiefs and empowering his loyal civilian deputies to eliminate bureaucratic resistance.[86] After the attacks of September 11, 2001, this same civilian control extended to operational planning for the wars in Iraq and Afghanistan. Military leaders got the message, and military dissent was essentially muzzled for the duration of Rumsfeld's tenure. Some parity would be restored to the civil-military dialogue only in the final quarter of the Bush presidency, when the NSC reasserted its authority relative to the vice president and Gates replaced Rumsfeld and sought to reinvigorate the JCS and Joint Staff.

Obama was elected promising a clean break from his predecessor's foreign policy. However, he inherited two wars and many simmering crises. His early presidency was marked by considerable friction between military officers who had been engaged in military conflict in Iraq and Afghanistan for eight years and newly arrived civilian appointees. Later in his presidency, seeking to closely monitor all military entanglements and potential escalations, Obama increasingly relied on his NSC staff for foreign policy formulation, leaving implementation to the Pentagon and the State Department.[87] Over time, this practice has prompted charges of micromanagement by NSC staff from agencies across the government. Senior White House advisors, meanwhile, argue that this is the only way to keep U.S. foreign policy in check and the best way to prevent leaks while the president considers his options.[88]

The prevailing lesson to draw from this history is that the system is never perfect. Leaders representing different ends of a three-million-person bureaucracy will always find compromise difficult. There is no national security structure that will make everyone happy—only a cooperation that gets the job done. The system breaks down when civilian and military leaders descend into open conflict or when one side acquiesces to the other and withholds advice. Truman's firing of MacArthur is a historical example of the former, Johnson and McNamara's taming of the joint chiefs during the Vietnam War is an example of the latter. The civil-military dialogue is at its worst when there is either too much friction or too little.

TOO MANY TEAMS OF TOO MANY RIVALS

Senior leaders can spend decades coming up the ranks of their respective institutions. These institutions—whether the military, a civilian agency, or the personal network of the president—shape leaders' interests and worldviews. Although the national security team may be united in its desire to serve the nation, its members will often hold vastly competing visions of what this looks like. Potential partners can become adversaries, each safeguarding its side and its interests. As the system slides toward paralysis, the atmosphere becomes one of profound mistrust.

This mistrust can prompt agencies to retreat to their corners as civilian and military officials begin to view even routine interactions with suspicion. This divide worsens as one travels further down the chain of command. Subordinates inevitably take cues from their supervisors. They become less likely to volunteer information to their interagency counterparts, nor do they feel empowered to discuss issues for which they lack explicit direction. IPCs and sub-IPCs transform into tiresome reiterations of institutional positions as officials fear getting ahead of their bosses. This not only can limit creative options development but also will inevitably disrupt the deliberative process, forcing decisions of even minor consequence to be made at the level of DC or above. According to a former high-level NSC appointee, "Clausewitz said that war is like 'running in water,' but if you add mistrust, it's like running in molasses."[89]

In their attempts to jumpstart policy discussions or disassociate themselves from a decision they disagree with, frustrated officials can resort to leaks, airing dirty laundry in the press. For the military, even the implied threat of a leak can serve as a powerful veto threat. A former high-level NSC appointee in the George W. Bush administration described how Bush agonized over a possible humanitarian intervention to halt an unfolding genocide in the Darfur region of Sudan. However, military advisors refused to discuss potential military options until they had been issued a formal tasking—something civilian officials assumed would then be immediately leaked to the media. The tasking never came.[90]

Meanwhile, military officials fear leaks of a different sort. All it takes is one hypothetical option, reportedly mentioned by one military advisor, to trap the Pentagon into undertaking a potentially risky course of action. Military officials are loath to have their remarks twisted into a widely held impression that a given option has been endorsed by the military establishment. The fear of such political maneuvering—what one former official describes as "hiding behind the skirts of the military"—can drive Pentagon representatives to raise their guard in low-level NSC meetings.[91] In a low-trust environment, leaks substitute for dialogue. According to a former combatant commander, the debate over military options can just as easily be "fought out through a series of leaks" as discussed around a conference table.[92]

In such an atmosphere of mistrust, civilian officials on the NSC may resort to what the military sees as micromanagement. Worried about second-order effects and even the slightest potential deviation from message, NSC staffers can take matters into their own hands, assuming the roles of civilian commanders instead of coordinators. Real-time videoconference, surveillance video streams, and instant communication with subordinate and tactical commands allow White House staff to circumvent higher levels of the military bureaucracy. More than one former combatant commander described how his command was bombarded with taskings from NSC staff that often bypassed the Pentagon.[93]

Military leaders, uncomfortable dispensing operational information or advice so informally, are inclined to request the NSC staffer go through formal taskings with their request. This means having the president task the secretary of defense, who then tasks the combatant commander, in a cumbersome chain for what might be small requests for information. Other officers, recognizing that this formal process can take more time than the NSC staffer probably has before going into an internal meeting with the national security advisor or the president, may instead decide to provide their best military advice on the spot. The risk here is that they will get ahead of other dialogue or analysis happening in the Pentagon.[94]

As the NSC staff devotes more resources to delving into tactical issues of military operations, Pentagon leaders can become frustrated. The secretary of defense and the chairman of the JCS, feeling distrusted, second-guessed, or bypassed by White House leadership, will be inclined to show more distrust in turn. Former Secretary of Defense Gates captures this sentiment in his description of civil-military friction at the commencement of the 2011 military intervention in Libya:

> I was . . . at the end of my tether with the White House-[NSC] micromanagement. The same day the military campaign began, I started to get questions at a principals' meeting with Donilon and Daley [national security advisor and White House chief of staff] about our targeting of Libyan ground forces. I angrily shot back, "You are the biggest micromanagers I have ever worked with. You can't use a screwdriver reaching from D.C. to Libya on our military operations. The president has given us his strategic direction. For God's sake, now let us run it.[95]

Together, these symptoms of mistrust—lack of transparency, leaks to the press, and pervasive micromanagement—can grind productive civil-military dialogue to a halt.

An example was seen in the first months of the Obama administration, as a new president and team of civilian advisors were expected to dictate policy for the Afghanistan war to military commanders who had been fighting it for eight years. These commanders, having conducted recent assessments of the Afghanistan war effort and already determined the need for more troops, grew increasingly frustrated with their civilian leadership as months ticked by. Meanwhile, Obama felt that he was being "jammed" by generals eager to "box him in" on a specific force level.[96]

The trouble began almost immediately upon Obama's entry into office. Both the overall commander in Afghanistan and Army General David Petraeus, commander of CENTCOM, presented a proposal, endorsed by Admiral Michael Mullen, chairman of the JCS, calling for the deployment of 30,000 additional troops in the theater.[97] Although this figure was the result of significant study that began under George W. Bush, it blindsided the newly arrived Obama appointees. As a handful of senior military officers on the NSC expressed their own doubts about the calculations involved, the White House felt justified in rejecting it.

A new review determined an "immediate" need for only 13,000 troops, but the NSC staff requested that these numbers be run again. This angered Mullen, who retorted that, "We're in charge of the numbers. We've got the numbers. We've done our homework."[98] So Gates commissioned another estimate that returned a higher number: 17,000. Obama ultimately approved 17,000 troops plus an additional 4,000 after further study. However, an atmosphere of suspicion had settled in between the White House and the Pentagon only a few months into the administration; vigorous debate over troop levels drowned out substantive discussion over actual strategy.[99]

Tensions simmered in the summer and fall of 2009 as Obama oversaw a reassessment of Afghanistan strategy. Ultimately, the military provided three options to the president: 20,000 for the "hybrid" counterterrorism model, 40,000 for a counterinsurgency variant, and 85,000 for a robust counterinsurgency variant.[100] The call for 85,000 troops was a political nonstarter; the uniformed military immediately threw its support behind 40,000. Mullen and Petraeus designed a high-level war game to test the 40,000 versus 20,000 options, but other military advisors urged the NSC to boycott, seeing the military's result as a foregone conclusion.[101] Obama convened a meeting with the joint chiefs, telling them bluntly: "I have one option that was framed as three options. I want three real options to choose from."[102]

Gates, sensing how toxic the civil-military dialogue had become, worked to find a compromise option of 30,000 troops, plus 4,500 enablers and an overall 10 percent flexibility based on circumstances on the ground.[103] Obama noted that even this compromise pushed the likely deployment above 36,000 and that the military was "really cooking the thing in the direction they wanted."[104] The president ultimately authorized 30,000. Even after this order, defense officials pressed for clarification or renegotiation of many parts of the order, which seemed to NSC staff as if the Pentagon was were disregarding a presidential directive.[105] Obama, frustrated by these perceived attempts to usurp his authority, personally devoted a day to dictating a precise, five-page order—a level of detail virtually unheard of in modern presidential directives.[106]

This episode combined many of the worst aspects of civil-military friction. White House advisors, many culturally unfamiliar with the military, were prompted to view the Pentagon with suspicion as their troop estimates came into question, while military leaders increasingly vented their own frustrations in public. Although the president had expected a range of military options, he received just three courses of action, and only one "real" choice. Pentagon planning was a black box to most White House staff, while top-level Afghanistan strategy meetings took place without any military leaders present. Although all parties sought success in Afghanistan, they lacked a shared vision and were never on the same side.

GROUPTHINK

Just as the civil-military dialogue can be paralyzed by too much friction, it can also be jeopardized by too little. This phenomenon falls broadly under the label of groupthink: the tendency of decision-making groups in high-stress, high-stakes environments to strive for unanimity at the expense of collective, creative inquiry. In his pioneering work on the subject, psychologist Irving Janis identified seven characteristics of groupthink:

- Group discussion limited to only a handful, usually two, courses of action;
- Failure to agree upon the fundamental objective and implied values of that objective;
- Failure to consider a preferred course of action's second-order effects and drawbacks;
- Negligence in revisiting courses of action initially dismissed as unsatisfactory;
- Failure to adequately assess the real losses and gains expected from each course of action;
- Selective bias toward new facts and information that support a preferred course of action; and
- Failure to develop credible contingency plans should the preferred course of action fail.[107]

The classic cases of groupthink are characterized by a lack of dissenting voices or alternative ideas. Applying the groupthink lens to foreign policy, Janis argued that many historical U.S. fiascoes occurred not because of inadequate information but because consensus was valued more highly than candor. The Bay of Pigs invasion was predicated on a plan whose details were never seriously vetted. Likewise, Johnson, McNamara, and others continually escalated the Vietnam War because, in each decision, they agreed that the choice was between doing more and losing outright—so they never saw a choice at all.[108]

Groupthink occurs in decision-making groups with low levels of friction and can occur at both low and high levels of team cohesion. Members of high-cohesion groups, seeking to avoid friction, will hesitate to voice objections for fear of disrupting group harmony. Meanwhile, members of low-cohesion groups will avoid challenging a prevailing idea for fear of being ostracized. In time, regardless of the level of cohesion, groupthink can foster the illusion of invulnerability among group members, a growing reliance on stereotypes, and even the emergence of self-appointed "mindguards" who neutralize inconvenient bits of information before they arise for debate.[109]

In the civil-military dialogue, groupthink can emerge when civilian leaders feel uncomfortable questioning military advice. Although this is essentially the Huntington ideal—an impermeable barrier between policy and action—it does not make for good decisions. Military advisors may possess an imposing knowledge of the mechanics of warfare, but they are not expected to consider the diplomatic, economic, and political consequences of their recommendations. In the words of a former secretary of defense, "Just because someone has a uniform doesn't make them smarter."[110]

However, the more dangerous form of groupthink occurs when civilian leaders misinterpret the strictures of civilian control to essentially run the Pentagon by force, actively quashing military dissent. In response, the military may self-censor. The textbook case of such groupthink is chronicled in H.R. McMaster's *Dereliction of Duty*, as the JCS under Kennedy and Johnson were gradually conditioned to withhold their candid assessments of the Vietnam War, instead committing to the same long game played by the politicians. According to McMaster, this failure to deliver uncomfortable military advice to the White House constituted a dereliction of duty at the highest levels of the Pentagon.[111]

A more recent example of such failure can be found in the planning process that preceded the 2003 invasion of Iraq. Rumsfeld entered office determined to leave his mark on the Pentagon. He was distrustful of the uniformed leadership, all holdovers of the Clinton administration.[112] He set out to upend the "Pentagon bureaucracy" and chose, as the new chairman of the JCS, a general with whom he had a "mind meld."[113] Rumsfeld boasted a decades-long relationship with Cheney, whose office had largely supplanted the role of the formal NSC, and many of Rumsfeld's civilian deputies felt empowered by their ties to both men.[114] All of these factors enabled Rumsfeld to neutralize institutional resistance to his reform measures, including his insistence on a strategy reliant on radically smaller and lighter ground forces.

As the Pentagon prepared plans for the Iraq invasion, Rumsfeld drove the process, working directly with the CENTCOM commander, General Tommy Franks, and largely co-opting the role of the Joint Staff. Rumsfeld embedded civilian deputies directly in the CENTCOM planning staff.[115] He carried on a "constant negotiation" with Franks over the size of the planned troop deployments, shifting the long-standing war plan of 385,000 to a force of 145,000, with 130,000 in reserve.[116] As the invasion drew closer, Rumsfeld ordered CENTCOM planners to do without a time-phased forces-deployment list, as he was dissatisfied with the size requirements calculated by the computer program.[117] While this dialogue included both uniformed military and civilians, it was also one-sided and dysfunctional.

Although Bush administration rhetoric implied that a goal of the Iraq War would be Iraqi democratization, Franks explicitly defined the end state as regime change.[118] Planning for Phase IV operations after this regime change was cursory and ignored long-standing planning and war-game results. CENTCOM was instructed to begin stability planning only in August 2002, while planning for postwar recovery and civil governance started at the beginning of 2003 with an untrained staff of fewer than one hundred.[119]

This incongruity of objectives and scarcity of resources went largely unchallenged by senior military leaders. In a January 30, 2003, meeting of the joint chiefs and president, all but the Army Chief of Staff General Eric Shinseki, endorsed the plan.[120] Shinseki, who believed that the proposed stabilization mission would require a force of between 350,000 and 500,000, repeated this assessment in public testimony shortly before the invasion.[121] Rumsfeld publicly repudiated Shinseki's assessment; Shinseki was marginalized by the other JCS members and ultimately forced into early retirement.[122] In the Rumsfeld Pentagon, groupthink won the day. The result, demonstrated in Iraq's rapid, postwar deterioration, was a force inadequately sized and postured to confront the challenges it faced.

Toward an Iterative
Civil-Military Dialogue

"It is always right to probe."
—Winston Churchill, as quoted in *Supreme Command*

Few terms are more popular in Washington policy circles than "iterative." In an ideal world, interagency partners gather to have iterative discussions. Each contribution builds atop the last, producing policies that are greater than the sum of their parts. The results are smart, novel, and iterated.

But even when the system works, this is not really what happens. The president will rarely begin deliberations equipped with the knowledge to build toward an agreed-upon objective, absent an understanding of the costs that each possible action might carry. Actual iteration can only begin once civilian policymakers and military advisors have had a more fundamental conversation. Because of cultural and institutional barriers, this discussion will invariably generate friction and discomfort. Yet, it needs to occur for the president to make the wisest possible decisions.

Although some aspects of the civil-military dialogue are essentially immutable, certain basic changes can remake the whole system for the better. The most important of these are empathy and empowerment. If each side understands the position of the other, civil-military interactions can shift from uncomfortable negotiations to frank conversations. Meanwhile, as subordinates feel empowered to take independent action, they will be more comfortable stepping away from institutional positions. Ultimately, civilians will feel more confident questioning military options, while military advisors will feel able to discuss the general limits of military capabilities without referring the question to a lengthy planning process.

Such dialogue is not without friction—but that is also the point. As Irving concluded at the end of his study of groupthink, "Healthy discussions sometimes become heated, especially when assumptions, failures, and omissions are examined. Nonetheless, they must be encouraged, and the occasional flare of a temper must be expected and tolerated."[123] A former NSC senior staffer echoes this observation: "My experience at State [Department] and the White House is that the best policy ideas come out of relaxed conversation, where people can say when something's a terrible idea."[124]

The importance of this basic sense of teamwork can get lost amid the complexity of the national security bureaucracy and the challenges it confronts.

FRICTION BY DESIGN

Sixty years after Huntington's famous treatise, the idea of the soldier as a quiet, aloof professional remains as attractive as ever. As the military continues to internalize its painful experiences in Iraq and Afghanistan, it could easily gravitate toward a new version of the Powell Doctrine—a clear division of civilian and military spheres and a road map to govern when military force should be used at all.[125] In this outcome, the Pentagon might take steps to guard its planning processes even closer, vigilant against the civilian meddling that has committed it to so many recent interventions abroad.

Such a move would be at odds with reality. Thanks to rapid changes in the international security environment, the future will hold more simmering crises like the civil war in Syria and fewer discretely military operations. The traditional planning process—premised on clear strategic guidance and weeks of lead time—will not be up to the task. Regardless of the party in power and the personalities of officeholders, the complexity of world events will require a collaborative relationship between senior civilian and military leaders.

This collaborative relationship does not have to be warm and fuzzy. Eliot Cohen's *Supreme Command* concluded that conflict functioned best in an "unequal" dialogue, where military opinions were expressed but not always heeded. Cohen criticized the Huntington ideal of a clear dividing line between civilian and military functions:

Where the "normal" [Huntingtonian] theory goes awry is in its insistence on a *principled*, as opposed to a *prudential* basis for civilian restraint in interrogating, probing, and even in extremis, dictating military action. Taken to extremes, it would free politicians of real responsibility for the gravest challenges a country can face, and remove oversight and control from those whose job most requires it.[126]

The alternative, a more interrogative civilian leadership and more forthright military advisors, invariably produces friction. Cohen describes this as a "conflictual, collaborative relationship, in which the civilian usually (at least in democracies) has the upper hand. It is a conflict often exacerbated by differences in experience and outlook . . . These differences are not ideological but temperamental, even cultural."[127] As long as these differences do not lead to the bureaucratic equivalent of lines drawn in the sand, they can enrich the process by which strategies are debated and decided. By expecting and accommodating a degree of friction, the national security system also avoids the groupthink that arises when friction is absent (see figure 1).

FIGURE 1. UNDERSTANDING FRICTION AND TEAM COHESION IN THE NATIONAL SECURITY SYSTEM

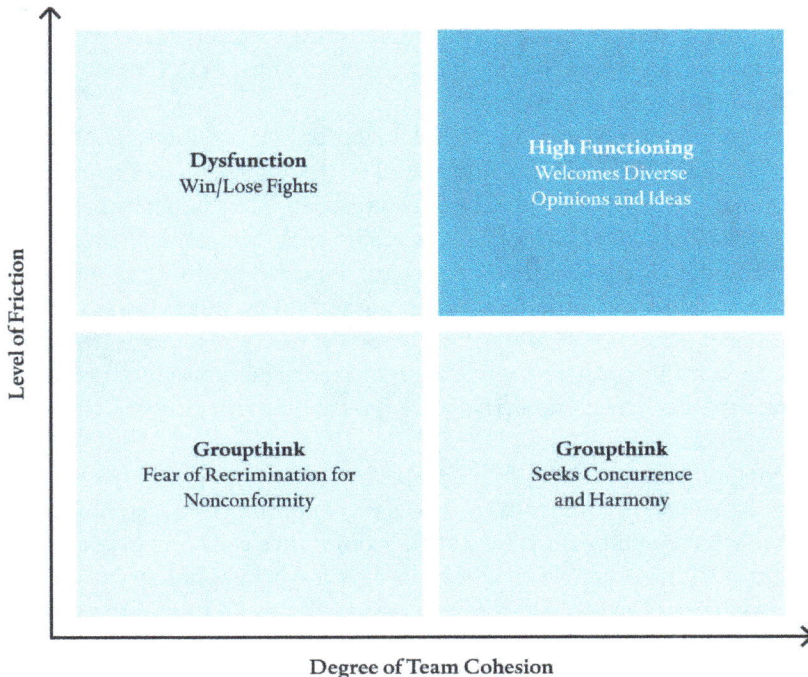

Source: Compiled by authors.

Teams that strive to avoid friction entirely can fall victim to group-think, regardless of their level of cohesion. Conversely, if friction manifests in a team with low levels of cohesion, its members will become more concerned with winning debates and building personal status than with solving the problem at hand. The challenge is to find the place where respectful debate among diverse but highly cohesive team members is encouraged but not to the extent that friction might undermine cohesion and stymie decision-making. The upper right quadrant of figure 1 depicts such a case: high-friction, high-cohesion, and high-functioning. In reengineering the national security system, this should be the goal.

EMPATHY AND EMPOWERMENT

A system designed to accommodate a certain amount of friction should also take strides to ensure that all agencies feel like they are on the same team. This can be accomplished by fostering a sense of empathy for interagency counterparts and ensuring the empowerment of subordinates so that they are not chained to the orthodoxy of their own institution. Doing so also requires patience, adopting incremental steps in this direction while appreciating that a three-million-person bureaucracy will not transform overnight.

A good example can be found in retired Army General Stanley McChrystal's five-year transformation of the Joint Special Operations Command (JSOC). As McChrystal writes, in its fight against loosely networked al-Qaeda cells, JSOC's traditional, hierarchical organization could no longer keep up.[128] Although individual JSOC teams were efficient, there was little integration among them, much less with the broader interagency community. Operators rarely saw value from the intelligence they gathered, while analysts struggled to produce products of tactical use. The components were fine, but the machine was sluggish and inefficient.

McChrystal sought to build empathy among the JSOC teams and their interagency counterparts through two initiatives. First, he established what could be described as the conference call from hell: a mandatory videoconference that ran six days a week, could stretch more than two hours, and boasted roughly seven thousand participants from numerous agencies. Each team member tasked with giving an update was also expected to answer questions that would not only explain facts and figures but also rationalize why the team had taken the action it had. Although time-consuming, this system served to keep JSOC members aware and involved with what otherwise invisible parts of the organization were doing. In order to push this awareness further, JSOC also designated liaison officers to interface across the organization and the government. According to McChrystal, "We didn't need every member ... to know everyone else; we just needed everyone to know someone on every team."[129]

Parallel with this new organizational empathy, what McChrystal calls "shared consciousness," JSOC also implemented "empowered execution," devolving authority enough that subordinates could feel comfortable making split-second decisions to exploit an intelligence opportunity without waiting for formal approval. As McChrystal explains, "In the old model, subordinates provided information and leaders disseminated commands. We reversed it: we had our leaders provide information so that subordinates, armed with context, understanding, and connectivity, could take the initiative and make decisions."[130] The result was a seven-thousand-person military command that acted with the situational awareness and speed of a much smaller organization.

While the JSOC transformation proves an impressive case study, it is not a perfect model for the wider national security system. The JSOC was a wartime command whose principal mission—defeating al-Qaeda—was never in question. Furthermore, although empowered execution sounds appealing, many restrictions exist to ensure that personnel abide by legal authorities and statutory divisions of power—important for a nation that exercises civilian control of the military. Nonetheless, McChrystal's model offers many lessons for the interagency planning and advisory process.

For the less agile and exponentially larger national security system, empathy begins with basic education and familiarization. Whereas large corporations regularly invest millions in team-building consultants and exercises, senior military and civilian leaders in the U.S. government are often introduced to their interagency partners only when a crisis emerges. It is simply unrealistic to assume this group of professionals, whose career paths and institutions are dissimilar, will immediately be able to function as a team to develop a shared consciousness or understanding of the problem. Instead, empathy can be cultivated by convening people who would likely work together in a crisis before such crisis happens, and giving them a chance to meet under more casual circumstances. In time, empathy imparts a degree of transparency and candor to otherwise stilted interactions. As a former vice chairman of the JCS observed, "You don't understand someone until you have a beer with them."[131] While such empathy cannot be dictated or engineered, it can be encouraged by providing frequent team-building exercises and opportunities.

Recommendations

Improving the civil-military dialogue requires changes to processes within and across the White House and the Pentagon, along with a focus on team-building and individual education and training. Thanks to different cultural and institutional drivers, civil-military relations will never lack friction; the trick is to promote healthy friction. Dynamism and respectful debate among diverse civilian and military team members—not groupthink—will produce better military options and advice.

Recommended changes include revising military planning doctrine, establishing standing interagency working groups, creating new options planning processes across both the Pentagon and the national security system, and introducing technology improvements that will make interagency coordination and communication more efficient. These reforms are interrelated. Changing planning processes at the interagency level, for instance, will have little effect without also adjusting leader expectations, doctrine, and training within and across agencies.

Gradually, these improvements to tone, team-building, and procedure will enable deeper institutional reforms intended to outlast a presidential administration. Future military leaders, as well as military planners and operational staff, should be taught a more nuanced concept of the civil-military dialogue that looks beyond Huntington's objective control. The next generation of Foreign Service officers should learn, earlier and in greater detail, how their military partners complement the work of U.S. diplomacy abroad, and the military should be taught how to translate technical military information into cogent advice that supports civilian decision-making.

Finally, and most ambitiously, civilian universities and colleges should be encouraged to offer more practical education in the field of national security: classes on deterrence, coercive diplomacy, war theory, and, critically, civil-military relations. Just as military officers should become more involved in the military options formulation process, civilian leaders should arrive in office equipped with better knowledge of the institutions they are expected to manage and of the driving theories associated with the use of military force. Changes in education will promote generational change, but steps can be taken today to set the course and improve decision-making now.

CLOSE THE KNOWLEDGE GAP

Although it is the military's responsibility to craft options in a format civilian leaders can understand, translating detailed operational information in a crisis situation would be smoother if the knowledge gap between military planners and civilian policymakers, including the president, were narrowed. Deployment timelines, sustainment logistics, the size and capability of an infantry battalion compared to a Navy SEAL team, or the real physical effects of a precision Tomahawk missile are not common knowledge. Although some senior civilian appointees have previous military experience, most do not. Thus the following recommendations are designed to better equip an incoming president and senior civilian advisors for their roles in the civil-military dialogue by providing them with relevant understanding of military affairs and capabilities.

- *Develop a Hands-On Program to Familiarize Civilians with the Military.* Civilian appointees are well versed in their own responsibilities, but many civilians interviewed admitted to feeling frustrated by the military's language and planning assumptions. As soon as possible, new civilian appointees should be offered a familiarization program on military issues, capabilities, and structures. This goal can be accomplished by scheduling visits to ships or bases, during which civilian and military leaders might observe military exercises and have in-depth discussions.
- *Dispel Myths.* Media and Hollywood images reinforce various incorrect and unrealistic stereotypes and beliefs about the types of high-tech capabilities the military may or may not possess. To counter unrealistic expectations, reference materials including fact sheets, briefing slides, and even short films could be developed to depict real-life military capabilities and operations. Virtual games might also allow decision-makers to explore the deeper trade-offs and opportunity costs when deciding among various military options in a resource-constrained environment.

BUILD AN EFFECTIVE
NATIONAL SECURITY TEAM

Effective teams do not emerge organically. As McChrystal's experience demonstrates, leaders need to set positive conditions for team-building at all levels. The following recommendations require direction and resources from the president and other White House leaders to achieve the vision of effective interagency teamwork in support of presidential decision-making.

- *Dedicate Time and Energy to Team-Building.* The overriding recommendation among those interviewed for this study is that NSC staff, mid-level political appointees—at the assistant secretary level and above—and senior military advisors in the Joint Staff would benefit from a series of team-building exercises including, ideally, weekend retreats involving flag officers and senior civilians from the White House, the Pentagon, and the intelligence community.[132] This team-building would include model DC and IPC meetings, Joint Staff planning sessions, and tabletop exercises. There would be an opportunity for role reversal: civilians could serve as military advisors while uniformed officers could role-play civilian policymakers, challenged to meet the president's interests with minimum guidance and information.

- *Continue to Practice.* Even after a presidential transition, the national security team continues to shift as positions are created, eliminated, or radically redefined and individuals depart or join. Recognizing the steep challenges of calendar management, civilian appointees and their military counterparts at the IPC level and above should commit to quarterly team-building events such as half-day tabletop exercises, site visits to military facilities, or other opportunities to build knowledge of the broader national security system and foster team cohesion, away from the high-stakes, zero-tolerance atmosphere that accompanies real-life security crises.

- *Set Up Interagency Working Groups.* To support options development in the short term and generational change over time, team-building should extend beyond senior civilian and military leaders. Mid-level action officers, regional experts, and military planners focused on particular regions or issues should meet regularly, talk through potential contingencies in their area of focus, and build relationships. As participants grow to trust one another, they often speak more freely. If and when a crisis occurs in their shared area of responsibility, these professionals will have a start in developing shared consciousness of the problem as they support the decision-making and options development processes for their bosses. Although such interagency working groups offer one of the best sources for predicting and preparing for future crises, participation is often undermined by competing priorities internal to each agency. Cultivating such a collaborative environment requires clear direction from senior leaders, who should sanction the establishment of such groups via interagency memoranda of understanding and reinforce the message to subordinates that their participation in the forum is a priority and an expectation of their professional portfolios.

SET THE TONE OF CIVIL-MILITARY DIALOGUE

Informal relationships and communication can provide the mortar between the "bricks" of the formal interagency structure. Military and civilian officials at all levels need to feel empowered to share information in order to explore new ideas and develop best options for the president. The following recommendations may at first be uncomfortable to officials accustomed to more hierarchical processes, but will, if adopted, enhance teamwork and trust through the promotion of free-flowing communication.

- *Distinguish Between Tasking and Communication.* Numerous military officers interviewed expressed exasperation at the tendency for NSC and OSD staffers to "jump the chain of command" by calling senior officers directly to ask for information. Understandably, these military leaders are reluctant to provide information that is potentially out of context or that may, upon further analysis, prove insufficient or out of sync with their superiors. For civilians, however, this seems a perfectly normal way to communicate and, indeed, provides a critical resource when their own bosses need information quickly. When there is not time to generate an official tasking or request for information from the president to the

Pentagon, this type of communication will need to suffice. Military officers should feel empowered by their leaders to offer their best professional advice and intuition while also conveying the need to confirm details through further, official inquiry. Meanwhile, the civilian staffer needs to understand that a general on a planning staff in a CCMD may be able to provide notional ideas on what might be done but will not have up-to-the-minute information on readiness levels, trade-offs across regions, or other qualifying information that the president also needs to know. Military planners in search of clarity on taskings may also find such informal communications channels and relationships useful. Such informal communication is critical to building relationships and promoting shared understanding and should not be stifled. At the same time, these interactions should be seen as supplemental to, and not replacement for, official communication pathways.

- *Build a Permissive Interagency Environment.* If all decisions are expected to originate from the top of the chain of command, the system becomes grossly inefficient. Senior leaders will not have time to get everything done; the talents of subordinate staff will go unrecognized and unused. To foster trust and encourage critical thinking, senior leaders—the secretary of defense, service secretaries, combatant commanders, national security advisor, and the president—should empower subordinates to coordinate at multiple levels to develop comprehensive, and creative, options. This goal can be accomplished by demonstrating tolerance for unorthodox ideas and suggestions, even if they stray from the established party line. Doing so starts with actions as simple as a leader setting the expectation, through guidance and performance reviews, that subordinates will be not only allowed but also expected to work closely with their peers at other offices and agencies.

- *Lead by Example.* Personal relationships among senior leaders have an outsize effect on the health of the national security bureaucracy. If leaders clash, they cannot foster empathy and empowerment for their subordinates. When personal relationships break down entirely— as they did for several years between the secretaries of state and of defense under President Reagan—interagency coordination suffers immensely. Cordiality and teamwork will only flourish if they exist at the top.

REDESIGN THE MILITARY OPTIONS PROCESS

The mismatch in expectations between military officers and their civilian counterparts during the decision-making process can quickly spark frustration. Civilians want a robust, iterative dialogue and multiple options to help decide what should be done, while the military expects concrete, up-front guidance as the foundation for planning. Military emphasis on using the detailed planning process to develop military advice misses an important step—an iterative presentation of possible military options to inform civilian decision. The following recommendations provide the intellectual and procedural foundation for designing draft, or "first round," military options that can help civilians understand what might be possible, perhaps even before detailed military planning commences.

- *Agree on the Definition of a "Military Option."* Civil-military frustration can be minimized and communication can be enhanced by establishing general expectations of what constitutes a military option. For the president to have a fair understanding of what is generally possible, a first-round set of options need not include fully vetted and resourced war plans. Military planners should present multiple options that give the president a rough order-of-magnitude understanding of what is militarily feasible for the problem and what the trade-offs might be in resources required, risks, and opportunity costs. Appendix 1 provides a template that military advisors might consider. Such a framework should be written into military doctrine and taught in military education.

- *Develop New Processes and Doctrine for Military Support to Decision-Making.* There needs to be a new category of military planning designed to support presidential decision-making. This process would not replace traditional detailed military planning but precede it. It would allow for the development of less detailed options designed to inform an iterative civil-military dialogue at the start of the decision-making process. Such a process would emphasize the development of multiple options, including multiple, distinct outcomes and rough force packages that describe what is possible and at what cost and risk. Military doctrine should acknowledge and embrace the inherent differences between traditional war planning and decision-support planning, designed to help civilian leaders determine if and how the president should use force to advance national security objectives.

- *Establish Interagency Planning Options Cells to Assist the NSC.* Too often, NSC crisis coordination presumes a level of interagency trust and collaboration that does not exist. Furthermore, NSC staff directors take on extraordinary administrative responsibilities to convene ad hoc interagency meetings on a given subject. As an alternative, the NSC should establish interagency planning options cells (IPOCs), co-chaired by appropriate agency representatives at the deputy assistant secretary level and coordinated by a dedicated administrative staff. These IPOCs would meet regularly, not just when there is a problem to be solved, and stand ready to work with augmented members from functional or other agencies or departments in the event of a crisis. They would be managed by NSC staff and regularly report their findings to an IPC group at the assistant secretary level. Their structural model would be similar to that of the 2005 Iraq Policies and Operations Group (IPOG), which helped consolidate the numerous lines of interagency communication needed for Iraq's reconstruction during Operation Iraqi Freedom. The civil-military options cells proposed in the following recommendation would work closely with their corresponding IPOCs (see appendix 2).

- *Establish Civil-Military Options Development Cells Within the Pentagon.* Reforming military options formulation and supporting the proposed IPOC require all Pentagon planning components—the Joint Staff, the OSD, and relevant CCMDs—to convene earlier in the process. Each Pentagon component brings an important perspective: OSD provides policy insight by clarifying the problem the president is trying to solve, the Joint Staff provides global force management data and a bridge to individual services by identifying what can be done, and CCMDs provide specific concepts of operation, functional expertise, and regional insights to identify what might work. Although the simultaneous participation of so many components is difficult, the alternative is worse: spending weeks or months developing ill-considered or politically infeasible options. The deputy assistant secretary of defense for plans could be assigned to organize these groups using appropriate personnel from the OSD, the Joint Staff, and relevant CCMDs. The cells would provide a forum for officials working the regional and functional issues to collaborate and develop military options for senior defense leaders to consider. While this cell would complement and support the IPOC from the military side, civilian agencies such as the State Department, USAID, and the intelligence community might consider similar adjustments to their internal structures and processes.

FACILITATE INTERAGENCY COMMUNICATIONS

Regular communication and face-to-face dialogue yield trust, teamwork, and collaboration. However, administrative delays and incompatibilities impair interagency communications, which require time to resolve. From building access to stove-piped email exchanges or security clearance confusion, the interagency system often stands in its own way. As a result, government officials skip interagency coordination to complete other important but less administratively difficult tasks, which are often more relevant for promotion. To realize the potential of the other recommendations contained in this report, red tape needs to be cut and technology used to remove long-standing obstacles to interagency coordination.

A top-down effort is needed to eliminate the many barriers to interagency communication and coordination. National security leaders should: create a shared email directory; institute common badges to ensure faster facility access to one another's buildings; establish a single clearance registry that prevents the need to pass clearances for every physical meeting and allows officials to easily verify if an individual has a common compartmented access; and build classified computer chat rooms that work across all agencies and are native to each agency's computer network without requiring the installation of additional software.

Currently, officials in some agencies need to go to a separate room or even compete for access to scarce "Secret" or "Top Secret" terminals. Because some national security components that regularly operate at higher levels of classification (e.g., the NSC) are inclined to label most communications "Top Secret," even maintaining a simple email exchange can be administratively burdensome. As much as possible, access to classified communications terminals should be significantly expanded. Moreover, interagency partners should strive to avoid overclassification and to use the lowest classification appropriate in order to improve interagency coordination.

PLANT THE SEEDS OF FUTURE CHANGE

Senior civilian and military leaders bring various academic and professional experience to the decision-making process. While this diversity of perspective can be an antidote to groupthink, it can also promote frustration and dysfunction when expectations about the nature of military power or about the decision-making and planning processes themselves are severely mismatched or unrealistic. Generational improvements in interagency decision-making teamwork need to target these misperceptions at the source; this means changing the educational experience on both sides. The following recommendations are designed to provide the next generation with a more realistic understanding of military power and the presidential decision-making process to better prepare both civilians and the military for the roles they may one day play.

- *Revise Professional Military Education.* Professional military education (PME) refers to the military system of training, development, and schooling. Unfortunately, current PME reinforces unrealistic expectations about the planning process: both the degree of guidance the president will provide and the inviolable line between civilian policymakers and military actors. PME curricula should spend more time preparing mid-level officers for the unequal dialogue they will likely encounter. In particular, the military's advanced planning schools should encourage students to consider not only the operational aspects of a problem but also its political dimensions. Current planning exercises should be adjusted to require students to develop multiple options in accordance with the above recommendations. Such reform should also extend to the highest levels of the military hierarchy. Flag officers' Capstone and Pinnacle courses provide an excellent opportunity to administer classes specifically devoted to developing draft military options in a manner that helps the presidential decision-making process. These classes should combine elements of the proposed orientation program for NSC staff and mid-level appointees, including interviews with other agencies' leadership, simulated interagency tabletop exercises and IPCs, and a higher-level reading list focused on civil-military theory and the history of non-military institutions like the NSC.

- *Boost the Curriculum for New Foreign Service Officers.* Foreign Service officers (FSOs) are expected to help manage the civil-military dialogue at every level of coordination. These officials will attend only one primary school—the Foreign Service Institute (FSI)—and they will return to school far less regularly than their military counterparts. Unfortunately, the FSI's introductory and intermediate-level courses place minimum emphasis on the civil-military dynamic, or the role of military power in achieving national security and foreign policy objectives, even though Foreign Service officers will likely be thrust into positions of interagency authority early in their careers. As a senior State Department official explains, this introduction to the military and interagency orientation happens "on the job; we learn it in the embassy context, in-country, and take it with us."[133] However, the extent of these lessons can vary greatly based on the inquisitiveness of the diplomat and the embassy postings. Diplomats should develop a basic understanding of military power early in their careers. Accordingly, steps should be taken to shift the FSI curriculum toward an earlier and more thorough orientation to military affairs and the diplomat's role vis-à-vis military leaders, from the embassies abroad to the Washington IPOC. Doing so would aid collaboration among military planners and diplomats at all levels throughout their careers and, critically, pay dividends when the time comes to provide the president with advice on military options.

- *Increase National Security Education at Civilian Colleges and Universities.* Most civilians—even highly educated political appointees—will have minimal understanding of the U.S. military and national security affairs until the day they are nominated to an important office. Having perhaps confused the study of war and warfare with the advocacy of war or of militarism in general, civilian education regarding the nature of warfare, military history, coercive diplomacy, deterrence, and other such fields has atrophied significantly in the twenty-five years since the end of the Cold War. But in order to ensure future generations of well-informed civilian and military leaders, efforts should be made to restore such instruction to college and university curricula. In the words of McMaster, "Thinking clearly about the problem of war and warfare . . . is both an unfortunate necessity and the best way to prevent it."[134]

Conclusion

Today, the civil-military dialogue—split by institutional and cultural differences—is being outpaced by the speed of global events. In considering the use of military force for complex, emerging crises, presidents can no longer wait upon the slow-moving gears of the traditional military planning process, nor can civilians remain ignorant of questions of human resources or logistics that lie at the heart of modern national security debates. Through improved education, strong executive leadership, and changes to procedure and doctrine, the civil-military dialogue in support of presidential decision-making can be improved. The recommendations here, if implemented together, can promote shared understanding, open and trustful interagency communication, and ultimately, room to consider and debate more creative options to the many challenges the United States will face in the twenty-first century.

Appendix 1:
Anatomy of an Option

A common complaint among civilian policymakers is that military advisors too often present only one fully tested option or offer courses of action with only slight variation in resource and levels in order to achieve a single outcome. To ensure truly distinct options, the president should require options papers that include the following six elements: a problem statement; a concept of operation (ways); required resources (means); opportunity costs; underlying assumptions; and a decision timeline. The president should be presented multiple options that are distinct in either outcomes or ways—or both. In some cases, different options could have a similar military outcome but use different means and incur different costs and risks. For instance, one option might use drone strikes to target an enemy combatant, while another might use a special operations team.

The following elements can be presented as a matrix of options to facilitate comparison and discussion during NSC meetings. For many complex contingencies, military action alone may be insufficient to achieve the desired objectives. Still, the options the military develops should sufficiently outline the limits of what is militarily "doable" at what levels of effort and cost and over what time frame. This provides critical input for the greater interagency discussion and presidential decision-making.

- *Problem Statement*: The problem statement is the most important element and describes what problem the president is trying to solve. For military planners, this has typically constituted the outcome. However, this is less often the case in simmering crises, where definitive end states tend to be unreasonably costly or unrealistic. The process of determining the nature of the problem requires an iterative interagency dialogue that can help promote shared consciousness among civilian and military advisors.

- *Concept of Operation (Ways):* Concepts of operation generally describe what the military forces will do. Each course of action should clearly describe how the military operation will unfold and how the proposed sequence of events is expected to lead to the desired outcome.

- *Resources (Means):* The discussion of resources required should describe what the military needs in order to execute the option. This includes an overview of the specific capabilities, such as ships, aircraft, munitions, and numbers of troops, that will be required, noting if a supplemental budget request to Congress is necessary.

- *Opportunity Costs:* This section will explain, if applicable, how moving military capabilities in support of the chosen option will affect ongoing or future operations elsewhere. For example, moving reconnaissance planes or satellites from one region to another might mean reduced coverage in the original area, which may place troops or national interests at risk. Moving a carrier strike group from the Pacific to another part of the world may undermine the deterrence posture in Asia or limit the president's ability to respond to a subsequent crisis there. Although these may be acceptable trade-offs, the president should be provided enough information to give them full and conscious consideration.

- *Risk:* The risk discussion should cover the many "what ifs" that concern a president in assessing how the option might unfold. Questions may include the likelihood of the military mission to achieve anticipated outcomes and what factors—weather, enemy capabilities, allied support, and logistics—might undermine the mission.

- *Timeline:* Finally, the decision timeline lets the president know how soon a decision is needed before the option may need to change substantially. The reason for change could be an election in a crucial partner country, expected changes to battlefield conditions, weather, or other events such as expectations that adversaries will acquire new technology or equipment, as in the case of the introduction of advanced air defenses. Not making a decision over a certain timeline may forgo some options entirely, an opportunity cost of which the president should be aware.

Appendix 2:
The Interagency Planning Options Cell

This appendix outlines one possible structural reform to improve the development of options for responding to simmering crises: interagency planning options cells. Because form influences function and budgets are constrained, IPOCs could serve three purposes: removing administrative burdens from NSC staff directors for specific topics, better preparing senior leaders in each department and agency to ensure productive interagency meetings, and generating rough order-of-magnitude options for dealing with simmering crises. An IPOC may require additional resources but could leverage standing structures in the federal government to accomplish these tasks.

The current national security decision-making structure focuses heavily on coordination among departments but often fails to promote trust and collaboration. This occurs due to time constraints and the overwhelming responsibilities of departmental representatives to attend numerous NSC staff meetings—IPCs, DCs, and PCs—not necessarily a lack of desire or effort. Action officers work valiantly to figure out details, coordinate, and collaborate at sub-IPCs, which also have substantial constraints because the NSC staff directors running those meetings often work twelve-hour days for six or seven days per week.

HISTORICAL PRECEDENT

The proposed IPOC builds on the success of the 2005 IPOG, which facilitated NSC staff meetings and consolidated interagency updates and recommendations for departments and the NSC staff. The group combined ten working groups and an overall steering committee, covering issues from coalition management to rule of law to terrorist financing, each staffed by agency representatives who were expected to attend regularly. The IPOG was an NSC staff initiative administered by State Department contractors that removed many administrative burdens from NSC staff and department action officers. According to a former IPOG facilitator, "Everyone still had an actual job within their respective agencies. This allowed them to manage their respective agency's tasks while also managing to come to an interagency meeting and actually get something done."[135] As participants grew to know and trust their interagency counterparts, IPOG members felt more comfortable resolving small decisions internally, as well as providing and accepting critical feedback.

Crucially, a dedicated IPOG administrative staff ensured that "all information was going in the right direction," according to the former IPOG facilitator.[136] The staff handled the synchronization of meetings and calendars, the organization of read-ahead material, the production and prompt distribution of meeting minutes, the coordination of agreed-upon deadlines, and any difficulties regarding security clearances. Although these minutiae had no bearing on policy, they might otherwise have posed an insurmountable barrier to busy interagency members. The IPOG facilitator calculated the resulting improvements in interagency coordination, cooperation, and collaboration led to a 70 percent reduction in DC and PC meetings, allowing representatives to spend time on higher-level national security issues.[137]

IPOC STRUCTURE, MEMBERSHIP, AND FACILITIES

The success of the IPOC depends on including the right members and leadership with connections to the relevant departments and NSC staff. As the IPOCs would cover a major set of issues, including simmering crises, many members would likely be sub-IPC participants, but co-chairs would be deputy-assistant-secretary-level representatives drawn from the appropriate agencies. The IPOC members would be staffed by mid-grade officials with the appropriate subject matter expertise from all relevant organizations—typically field-grade military officers and General Service 14-15s. These should be the individuals who typically provide preparation materials for senior leaders attending NSC meetings. Overall, an NSC staff member would be responsible setting IPOC priorities, although the IPOC would largely work independently, given the NSC staff's limited bandwidth. The IPOC would always report

FIGURE A1. THE INTERAGENCY PLANNING OPTIONS CELL AND
THE NATIONAL SECURITY SYSTEM

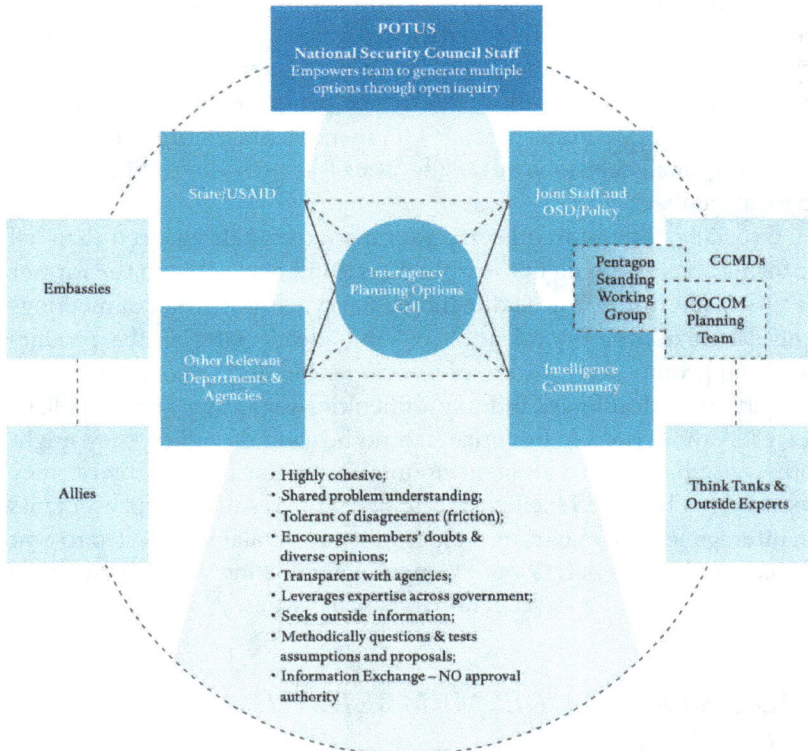

Source: Compiled by authors.

to the appropriate NSC staff desk officer, with each IPOC member
continuing to report to their home organization and preparing senior
leader representatives to the NSC.

All IPOCs would share a common standing administrative staff for
scheduling meeting space, providing information technology support
and scenario development, and facilitating planning sessions with idea
collaboration tools. The IPOC would need conference rooms in a location with connectivity to each organization's classified and unclassi-
fied computer networks, allowing easy communication with the parent
organization and preventing the need for people to rush back to their
offices, which would significantly increase participation.

STEADY-STATE COORDINATION

Each IPOC would gather no less than one day per month regardless of the NSC meeting schedule, with NSC director participation when possible. Access to their parent organization's computer networks would allow members to complete pressing requirements without departing and provide opportunities for informal collaboration throughout the meeting. Informal collaboration often leads to helpful insights and ideas that would not otherwise occur. During the day, IPOC members would have at least one session to discuss current issues, operations, and policy. These sessions would focus on developing trust among members and building a shared understanding of security concerns and the different problems faced by each organization.

The IPOCs would also gather for quarterly tabletop exercises at the staff level, providing the foundation for a semi-annual tabletop exercises conducted at higher levels and staffed by the working-level IPOC. One- or two-day tabletop exercises would focus on potential crises relevant to each IPOC and give members practice developing options collaboratively. In addition, IPOCs would gather before DC, PC, and NSC staff meetings to discuss each organization's perspective and help each member develop preparation material for their organization's representative. Collaborating across agencies at the working level in advance of more senior leader meetings would improve the quality of senior leader discussion by clarifying misunderstandings or exposing potential areas of disagreement for senior leaders to resolve.

Regardless of preparation, participants may leave NSC staff meetings with different perspectives of what occurred. The summary of conclusions provides the official version of events but often takes too long to produce by an overworked NSC staff. The IPOC would alleviate this problem by having IPOC staff remotely monitor DC, PC, and NSC meetings and immediately produce an initial draft summary of conclusions for review and adjustment by the NSC staff. Using the IPOC requires a culture of transparency and collaboration that may need to be built through practice. Over time, this transparency would improve shared understanding of problems across departments and lead to more collaborative options development.

CRISIS OPERATIONS

While steady-state IPOC operations have independent value, the IPOC's primary purpose is improving collaboration during those periods when a simmering crisis boils over and the president needs a wide range of options quickly. At this point, the IPOC would become a real planning cell, helping to develop and vet rough order-of-magnitude options across departments and agencies. The IPOC's ability to execute this function would depend on the trust established before the crisis. As a common government saying goes, "You can't surge trust"—trust being a critical commodity in times of emergency response.

During crisis, the IPOC would sequester itself in a common location to focus solely on developing options for the president, dropping other requirements. The full-time administrative staff would lead the IPOC through the planning process under the direction of the co-chairs or an alternate leader designated by the IPC or DC, likely the lead agency's IPOC representative. Regular communication with the appropriate NSC staff directors would help the process, but NSC staff directors lack the time to run lengthy brainstorming and options-development sessions. Therefore, IPOC members would need the authority to continuously reach back to their home organizations, including planning cells in the Pentagon, embassies, and other forward locations, to pull needed information ranging from resource requirements to platform capabilities to legal issues to expertise on significant foreign partners or adversaries. The IPOC members would need to have sufficient expertise to avoid frivolous questions or requests for readily available information.

Each IPOC-generated option would include a problem statement, a concept of operation, required resources, opportunity costs, underlying assumptions, and a decision timeline (see appendix 1). In military parlance, these rough options would resemble "Level 1" plans or a "commander's estimate" but some would purposefully explore alternate objectives and end states. The IPOC would fulfill its mission if it ensured presentation and consideration of multiple options, preventing the president from feeling unable to act.

The IPOC, as described, offers only a template. Its most important features are a dedicated administrative staff and technology-supported meeting area, a steady-state working group structure intended to support the NSC, and the empowerment of lower-level interagency representatives. Any structure that follows these basic principles will add immense value to the process of presidential decision-making.

Appendix 3:
Methodology and Acknowledgments

This report arises from Janine's thirty years of involvement with the U.S. national security establishment: as a confused junior Air Force officer; a professor and analyst of defense policy; and as a senior civilian appointee within the Department of Defense. It is informed by a close reading of military theory and relevant case studies, a series of focus groups with mid-level military planners, and a full-day workshop that convened national security officials from across a multitude of agencies.

The most important source of information came from one dozen structured, detailed interviews conducted with retired civilian and military leaders, each of whom has served at the highest levels of government. These included former national security advisors, secretaries of defense, combatant commanders, and senior members of the Joint Staff. Their names have been anonymized in this final report. We are grateful to these distinguished men and women for the time they gave us, as well as their continuing involvement in this study.

We would like to thank Michèle Flournoy, Peter Feaver, Nadia Schadlow, James M. Lindsay, and Richard N. Haass for their support of this investigation and their interest in our findings, as well as the Smith Richardson Foundation. Nancy Blacker, Nate Finney, Jim Golby, Scott Kendrick, and Troy Thomas aided greatly in the consultation and fact-checking that made this report possible. Finally, thanks to Amy Schafer, Zachary Austin, Sam Ehrlich, and Andrew Ziebell for their excellent research and administrative assistance.

Endnotes

1. Since 1980, roughly 70 percent of national and deputy national security advisors have hailed from legal or academic backgrounds.
2. Amy B. Zegart, *Flawed by Design: The Evolution of the CIA, JCS, and NSC* (Stanford University Press, 2000), p. 133.
3. Ibid, p. 3.
4. Ibid, p. 16.
5. Karen DeYoung, "How the Obama White House Runs Foreign Policy," *Washington Post*, August 4, 2015, http://washingtonpost.com/world/national-security/how-the-obama-white-house-runs-foreign-policy/2015/08/04/2befb960-2fd7-11e5-8353-1215475949f4_story.html.
6. "50 U.S.C. § 402: US Code - Section 402: National Security Council," *Findlaw*, accessed June 14, 2016, http://codes.lp.findlaw.com/uscode/50/15/I/402.
7. Zegart, *Flawed by Design*, p. 94.
8. Ibid, p. 80.
9. Ibid, 81.
10. David Rothkopf, *Running the World: The Inside Story of the National Security Council and the Architects of American Power* (PublicAffairs, 2009), p. 84.
11. Ibid, p. 404.
12. DeYoung, "How the Obama White House Runs Foreign Policy."
13. Rothkopf, *Running the World*, p. 269.
14. Former NSC staffer, interview by Janine Davidson, October 27, 2014.
15. Zegart, *Flawed by Design*, p. 99; Samuel P. Huntington, *The Soldier and the State: The Theory and Politics of Civil-Military Relations* (Cambridge: Belknap Press, 1981), p. 447.
16. Zegart, *Flawed by Design*, p. 140; Deborah Shapley, *Promise and Power: The Life and Times of Robert McNamara* (Little Brown & Co, 1993), p. 126.
17. Former national security advisor, interview by Janine Davidson, March 23, 2015.
18. Huntington, *The Soldier and the State*, pp. 318, 323.
19. Zegart, *Flawed by Design*, p. 136.
20. Ibid, p. 110.
21. Joint Staff structure is derived from the European general staff structure introduced in the mid-nineteenth century. The levels of J1 through J8 are: J1, manpower and personnel; J2, joint staff intelligence; J3, operations; J4, logistics; J5, strategic plans and policy; J6, C4 (command, control, communications, and computers) and cyber; J7, joint force development; and J8, force structure, resources, and assessment. "Joint Staff Structure," Joint Chiefs of Staff, accessed August 29, 2016, http://www.jcs.mil/leadership.
22. "Joint Publication 5-0: Joint Operation Planning, August 11, 2011," Joint Electronic Library, http://www.dtic.mil/doctrine/new_pubs/jointpub_planning.htm.

23. Former national security advisor, interview by Janine Davidson.

24. Mark Bucknam, "Planning Is Everything," *Joint Forces Quarterly* 62, 3rd quarter 2011, p. 55.

25. Former combatant commander No. 1, interview by Janine Davidson, August 27, 2015.

26. Former combatant commander No. 2, interview by Janine Davidson, December 17, 2014.

27. David Zucchino and David Cloud, "U.S. Military and Civilians Are Increasingly Divided," *Los Angeles Times*, May 24, 2015, http://latimes.com/nation/la-na-warrior-main-20150524-story.html.

28. Janine Davidson, "Civil-Military Friction and Presidential Decision Making: Explaining the Broken Dialogue," *Presidential Studies Quarterly* 43, no. 1, March 2013, p. 132.

29. Rothkopf, *Running the World*, p. 322.

30. Former NSC staffer, interview by Janine Davidson.

31. Huntington, *The Soldier and the State*, p. 7.

32. Ibid, p. 12.

33. Ibid, p. 68–69.

34. David Petraeus, *The American Military and the Lessons of Vietnam: A Study of Military Influence and the Use of Force in the Post-Vietnam Era* (Princeton University, 1987).

35. Caspar Weinberger, "The Uses of Military Power," speech given at the National Press Club, Washington, DC, November 28, 1984.

36. Eliot A. Cohen, *Supreme Command: Soldiers, Statesmen and Leadership in Wartime* (Simon and Schuster, 2012), p. 3.

37. Thomas E. Ricks, *The Generals: American Military Command from World War II to Today* (Penguin Group USA, 2013), p. 382.

38. Janine Davidson, telephone interview with Brigadier General (now Major General) William Hix, September 12, 2012.

39. Cohen, *Supreme Command*, p. 178.

40. Ibid, 201; Michael R. Gordon and Bernard E. Trainor, *Cobra II: The Inside Story of the Invasion and Occupation of Iraq* (Vintage Books, 2007), pp. 102–3.

41. Huntington, *The Soldier and the State*, p. 66.

42. Bob Woodward, *Obama's Wars* (Simon and Schuster, 2010), p. 280.

43. Gates, *Duty*, p. 424.

44. Michael Shekleton, "Risk Articulation and Options in War: Telling a Story," *The Bridge*, June 21, 2016, http://thestrategybridge.com/the-bridge/2016/6/21/risk-articulation-and-options-in-war-telling-a-story.

45. Janine Davidson, telephone interview with former Deputy Assistant Secretary of State James Steinberg, September 6, 2012; Davidson, "Civil-Military Friction and Presidential Decision Making," p. 143.

46. Former senior Joint Staff military planner, interview by Janine Davidson, January 7, 2015.

47. Former member of State Department policy planning, "Military Advisors Working Group" (Washington, DC, December 10, 2014).

48. Dwight D. Eisenhower, "Remarks at the National Defense Executive Reserve Conference," November 14, 1957.

49. "Joint Publication 5-0," Joint Electronic Library.

50. Matthew Gaetke, "Certainty Is Illusion: The Myth of Strategic Guidance," monograph from the School of Advanced Military Studies, 2015, http://cgsc.contentdm.oclc.org/cdm/ref/collection/p4013coll3/id/3432.

51. Former senior Joint Staff military planner, interview by Janine Davidson.
52. Former national security advisor, interview by Janine Davidson.
53. "Defense Headquarters: Guidance Needed to Transition U.S. Central Command's Costs to the Base Budget," Government Accountability Office, June 2014, p. 41.
54. Former national security advisor, interview by Janine Davidson.
55. John F. Troxell, "PDD 56: A Glass Half Full," in *The U.S. Army War College Guide to National Security Issues: National Security Policy and Strategy*, ed. J. Boone Bartholomees (Strategic Studies Institute, 2010); Nora Bensahel, Olga Oliker, and Heather Peterson, "Improving Capacity for Stabilization and Reconstruction Operations" (RAND, 2009).
56. Executive Office of the President of the United States, *The Clinton Administration's Policy on Managing Complex Contingency Operations*, PDD/NSC 56, 1997, http://fas.org/irp/offdocs/pdd56.htm.
57. Troxell, "PDD 56: A Glass Half Full."
58. William Hamblet and Jerry Kline, "Interagency Cooperation: PDD 56 and Complex Contingency Operations," *Joint Forces Quarterly*, Spring 2000, pp. 93–95.
59. Troxell, "PDD 56: A Glass Half Full," p. 76.
60. Executive Office of the President of the United States, *Management of Interagency Efforts Concerning Reconstruction and Stabilization*, NSPD 44, 2005, http://fas.org/irp/offdocs/nspd/nspd-44.html.
61. J.D. Hooker and Joseph Collins, "An Interview with Martin E. Dempsey," *Joint Forces Quarterly*, July 1, 2015.
62. Former senior Joint Staff military planner, interview by Janine Davidson.
63. Ibid.
64. Sean Carmody, "Planner's Role in the Civil-Military Relationship: Syrian Crisis Action Planning (2011–2013)," monograph from the School of Advanced Military Studies, 2015, p. 4, http://cgsc.contentdm.oclc.org/cdm/ref/collection/p4013coll3/id/3356.
65. Ibid, pp. 36–37.
66. Former senior Joint Staff military planner, interview by Janine Davidson.
67. Martin Dempsey, "Military Options with Regard to Syria; Letter to the U.S. Senate Armed Services Committee," *The Hill*, July 19, 2013, http://thehill.com/images/stories/news/2013/07_july/22/dempsey.pdf.
68. Ibid.
69. Andrew J. Bacevich, "Elusive Bargain: The Pattern of U.S. Civil-Military Relations since World War II," in *The Long War: A New History of U.S. National Security Policy Since World War II*, ed. Andrew J. Bacevich (New York: Columbia University Press, 2007).
70. Ibid, p. 24.
71. Rothkopf, *Running the World*, p. 88.
72. Bacevich, "Elusive Bargain," p. 32; H. R. McMaster, *Dereliction of Duty: Johnson, McNamara, the Joint Chiefs of Staff, and the Lies That Led to Vietnam* (New York: Harper Perennial, 1998).
73. Ricks, *The Generals*, p. 256.
74. Rothkopf, *Running the World*, p. 220.
75. Ibid, p. 229.
76. Former NSC staffer, interview by Janine Davidson.
77. Rothkopf, *Running the World*, pp. 245–49.
78. Ibid, p. 255.
79. Ricks, *The Generals*, pp. 375–76.

80. Bacevich, "Elusive Bargain," pp. 42–43.

81. Rothkopf, *Running the World*, p. 325.

82. Bacevich, "Elusive Bargain," p. 44.

83. Rothkopf, *Running the World*, p. 324.

84. Ibid, pp. 332–33.

85. Former ambassador, interview by Janine Davidson, March 24, 2015; "Mending the Broken Dialogue: Civil-Military Friction and Presidential Use of Force" (Washington, DC, October 22, 2015).

86. Gordon and Trainor, *Cobra II*, pp. 7–22.

87. Jeffrey Goldberg, "The Obama Doctrine," *The Atlantic*, April 2016, http://theatlantic.com/magazine/archive/2016/04/the-obama-doctrine/471525.

88. Glenn Thrush, "Obama's Obama," *Politico*, accessed January 7, 2016, http://politico.com/magazine/story/2016/01/denis-mcdonough-profile-213488.

89. Former NSC staffer No. 2, telephone interview by Janine Davidson, May 1, 2015.

90. Ibid.

91. Ibid.

92. Former combatant commander No. 2, interview by Janine Davidson.

93. This was a consistent theme across all interviews and conversations with former combatant commanders.

94. Former combatant commander No. 3, phone interview by Janine Davidson, September 9, 2015.

95. Gates, *Duty*.

96. Ibid.

97. Woodward, *Obama's Wars*, pp. 80–81.

98. Ibid, pp. 94–95.

99. Ibid, p. 114.

100. Ibid, p. 212–13.

101. Ibid, p. 244.

102. Ibid, p. 258.

103. Ibid, p. 308.

104. Ibid, p. 280.

105. Ibid, p. 314.

106. Ibid, p. 327.

107. Irving L. Janis, *Groupthink: Psychological Studies of Policy Decisions and Fiascoes* (Boston: Cengage Learning, 1982), p. 10.

108. Ibid.

109. Ibid, pp. 174–75.

110. Former secretary of defense, interview by Janine Davidson, June 4, 2015.

111. McMaster, *Dereliction of Duty*.

112. Gordon and Trainor, *Cobra II*, p. 7.

113. Ibid, p. 46.

114. Ibid, p. 39.

115. Ibid, p. 32.

116. Ibid, p. 28.

117. Ibid, p. 100.

118. Ibid, p. 67.

119. Ibid, p. 139; 142.

120. Ibid, p. 101.

121. Ibid, p. 102.

122. Ibid.

123. Janis, *Groupthink*, p. 383.

124. Former NSC staffer, interview by Janine Davidson.
125. Janine Davidson, *Lifting the Fog of Peace: How Americans Learned to Fight Modern War* (University of Michigan Press, 2010).
126. Cohen, *Supreme Command*, p. 13.
127. Ibid, p. 10.
128. General Stanley McChrystal et al., *Team of Teams: New Rules of Engagement for a Complex World* (New York: Portfolio, 2015).
129. Ibid.
130. Ibid.
131. Former vice chairman of the Joint Chiefs of Staff, "Mending the Broken Dialogue: Presidential Decision-Making and the Presidential Use of Force."
132. Former senior Joint Staff military planner, interview by Janine Davidson; "Mending the Broken Dialogue: Civil-Military Friction and Presidential Use of Force."
133. Senior State Department official, telephone interview by Janine Davidson, January 15, 2016.
134. H.R. McMaster, "The Warrior Ethos at Risk," speech given at Georgetown University, Washington, DC, November 11, 2014).
135. Former IPOG facilitator, interview by Emerson Brooking, August 25, 2015.
136. Ibid.
137. Ibid.

About the Authors

Janine Davidson is a former senior fellow for defense policy at the Council on Foreign Relations, where she is also a life member. From 2009 to 2012, she served as deputy assistant secretary of defense for plans, overseeing the formulation and review of military war plans and global force posture policy. Davidson has taught national security policy and political science at Georgetown University, George Mason University, and Davidson College. Her 2009 book, *Lifting the Fog of Peace: How Americans Learned to Fight Modern War*, examines organizational change and institutional learning in the U.S. military. Davidson began her career as a pilot in the Air Force. She holds a BS in architectural engineering from the University of Colorado at Boulder and a PhD in international studies from the University of South Carolina.

Emerson T. Brooking is a research fellow at the Council on Foreign Relations. He served previously as a research associate for defense policy, also at the Council on Foreign Relations. His work has been published in the *Atlantic*, *Foreign Policy*, and *Popular Science*, among others. He holds a BA in political science and classical studies from the University of Pennsylvania.

Benjamin J. Fernandes is assigned to U.S. Army Training and Doctrine Command. Lieutenant Colonel Fernandes has served previous tours of duty in Afghanistan, Europe, Korea, and Alaska. Fernandes holds a BS in international relations from the U.S. Military Academy, an MBA from Auburn University, and an MS in strategic intelligence from the National Intelligence University. He is pursuing a PhD at George Mason University and is a term member of the Council on Foreign Relations.

.

www.ingramcontent.com/pod-product-compliance
Lightning Source LLC
Chambersburg PA
CBHW052142270326
41930CB00012B/2986